REFLECTIONS
ON A
LITERARY REVOLUTION

Reflections

on a

Literary Revolution

GRAHAM HOUGH

Fellow of Christ's College, Cambridge

THE CATHOLIC UNIVERSITY OF AMERICA PRESS

WASHINGTON, D. C.

1960

In reprinting the lengthy prose passage and three complete poems quoted herein, the publishers make the following grateful acknowledgements: For the passage from the Introduction by T. S. Eliot to his translation of *Anabase* by St.-John Perse, to Faber and Faber, Ltd. (London), Harcourt, Brace and Company, Inc. (New York), and to Mr. Eliot himself, for their gracious permission to quote from this work and from his poems; for "To Earthward" by Robert Frost, quoted in full, to Henry Holt and Company, Inc. (New York); for "In a Station of the Metro" and "Fan-Piece, for Her Imperial Lord" by Ezra Pound, both quoted in full, to New Directions (New York).

iv

Preface

I had the honour to deliver these lectures at The Catholic University of America under the auspices of the Monsignor George A. Dougherty Foundation and the Department of English in the spring of 1959. They are an attempt to put together some general ideas on the poetic upheaval of the earlier part of this century. I start from the supposition that we have experienced a revolution as great as the Romantic one of a century before; and that the revolution is now over. We are just now, perhaps, in a position to ask ourselves what its nature was, and how it can be related to our previous literary experience.

Many among my audience plainly disagreed with what I had to say, and I would thank them for their kindly forbearance to my person in spite of their detestation of my opinions. While I was working on these lectures I was Visiting Professor at Cornell University, and I should like to offer my warmest thanks to my colleagues in the English Department there for many lively and illuminating discussions of the matters considered in these pages. Lastly, I wish to thank Professor H. E. Cain of the Department of English at The Catholic University for the considerable thought he took in arranging these lectures.

I.

Imagism and
Its Consequences

Literature, by a fortunate dispensation, does not
reflect very accurately the convulsions of the social
order. Its revolutions sometimes precede the social ones,
sometimes follow them, sometimes, it would seem,
overlap them quite pointlessly. In any case the cultural
historian has no difficulty in finding the relations he
is disposed to find. He deals in large masses of material,
the phenomena are so numerous that they can surely
be connected in more ways than the ingenuity of a
commentator can devise. But as soon as we begin to
look closely at a particular patch of literature we are
likely to see it developing according to its own principles, which have their own interest, and are likely to
be at least partly fortuitous in their relations to the
wars, technologies or movements of classes that are
their temporal accompaniments. The dispensation is
fortunate, for it is a happy instance of what we mean
by the freedom of the spirit.

Looked at in a sufficiently apocalyptic light, the
extraordinary outbreak of genius and novelty in the
literature of the early part of this century can be seen
as the response of the imagination to the appalling

moral and political history of our age. And so no doubt it is, and all the books with crisis, revolt, dilemma and hazard in their titles are right. But part of the imaginative response has always been to occupy itself with other things than crises and hazards. "I particularly admired your use of the pluperfect subjunctive" as Claudel once remarked to Gide. The imagination has its own procedures and its own stratagems, different for every art in which it expresses itself. In the visual arts and in music the devices may be of international range. In literature they can hardly be that, for each language has its own procedure, never held quite in common with that of any other. The closer we come to a particular literature the more closely its features will be seen to depend on the state of the language at the time, the state of previous writing in it, the prestige or the declining fortune of special forms. In short, a literary revolution must be a *literary* revolution if it is to be anything. It may accompany or be accompanied by almost any other kind of revolution, at almost any distance. But unless we are looking at literature as a symptom of something else (a possibly respectable occupation, but not that of the literary critic) what must be attended to is the behaviour of literature itself.

The years between 1910 and the second world war saw a revolution in the literature of the English language as momentous as the Romantic one of a century before. It is an Anglo-American development that is itself part of a whole European affair. Beside the names of Yeats, Joyce, Eliot and Pound we should wish to place those of Gide, Valéry and Thomas Mann, perhaps Proust and Rilke from an earlier generation. Here is our identification parade for the modern spirit in letters. But here too we have such a huge and various collective phenomenon that almost anything we care to say about it would be true of some part or other; the target is so large that any chance-aimed shot would be sure to hit it somewhere. If we look at it *en masse* we shall soon find ourselves speaking of crisis in Western values, of dissociation of sensibility, of alienation, and disinherited minds. Looking from this vertiginous height we shall surely be able to make many observations that are true, the more easily since they are not liable to the contradictions of particularity. Let us descend and recover balance by observing a fixed spot—London in the years just before 1914. It was there that the English cell of an almost worldwide poetic conspiracy was being incubated—the first plot against the literary establishment for over a hundred years. Of course foreign agents were at work; there had been correspondence with France and the Orient; a person from Idaho and one from St. Louis were actually present.

So in the next few years "modern poetry" came into being. Strangely, it is still modern poetry, the same article, sold under the same name. The revolution is long past. Of the central revolutionary quartet—Pound, Eliot, Joyce and Wyndham Lewis—"the men of 1914," as Lewis liked to call them (it is characteristic that the turn of phrase should be borrowed from European revolutionary politics) two are dead, one legally irresponsible, and the fourth is happily still with us, the greatest living man of letters. A generation has had to pass to bring about this change of aspect. But nothing has happened to dispute with their productions the title of modern letters. No *avant-garde* has advanced any farther. There is no *avant-garde*. When I was a boy "modern poetry" was to be distinguished from poetry simple. Poetry was inherited from parents and learnt at school; it was the "Ode on a Grecian Urn" and "The Solitary Reaper." Modern poetry was read in a different context; neither one's parents nor anyone at school knew anything about it. Modern poetry is now academically respectable. It is taught in college courses, and the exposition of it gives employment to many worthy persons. But it is still almost as distinct from "poetry" as ever. Distinct in the general imaginaton, and not only in that; even among those who seriously profess the arts there is a feeling of the discontinuity between the literature of our century and that of any previous one. The singularity of modern poetry, for example, is one of the arguments used by C. S. Lewis to support his hypothesis of a great rift in our culture just before the present age.

Imagism and Its Consequences

This consciousness of modernity is a distinctively modern thing; it is largely the work of the revolutionary generation itself. Pound's essays were called *Make It New*. In the stream of advice and exhortation he offered to young writers there is a continual insistence on novelty and on being up-to-date. "No good poetry is ever written in a manner twenty years old." "The scientist does not expect to be acclaimed as a great scientist until he has *discovered* something."[1] In both his and Eliot's criticism we are always hearing about "what remains to be done," "what is to be done next." A curious instance of this acute period-consciousness occurs quite recently, in Mr. Eliot's introduction to Pound's *Literary Essays*. He cites as one of the tricks of malevolent critics—"to quote what a writer said twenty or thirty years ago as if it was something he had said yesterday."[2] It is hard to imagine Johnson or Coleridge or Arnold finding it "malevolent" to quote a twenty-year-old dictum without the appropriate date. Lest I be suspected of malevolence may I add that the date of this remark is 1954, a date far removed from the dust of revolutionary conflict. Plainly the instigators of the late poetic innovation were badly frightened by a Zeitgeist, and the effects have been lasting.

The new poetry was new in the twenties, and it is still new, in the sense that we have nothing newer. As early as 1935 we find Sir Herbert Read, in an essay called *Form in Modern Poetry,* complaining of backsliding, of a decline in revolutionary and experimental ardour. It might be that the new tradition had established itself, that we now have a body of followers working in an accepted mode. But this is not true, or true only in a very restricted area. The revolution of 1914 was quite as momentous as the Romantic one of over a century before, but it was different. The Romantic change was not at all antipathetic to ancient and deep-rooted tendencies. In many ways it was a return to them; the old textbook term is after all the Romantic Revival. The result is that its habits of feeling and expression are a model for the next hundred years. The nineteenth-century shelves are stuffed with Wordsworthian poems, Keatsian poems and Byronic poems. The modern revolution has had a different fate. In one direction, in the establishment of a modern colloquial poetic idiom, the younger writers have certainly learnt the lesson of their elder contemporaries. All that purgation of poetic diction that has been so carefully and beautifully worked out, both in theory and in practice, by Mr. Eliot has become an almost absolute critical rule. The rule has been formulated, with something less than complete approval, in a recent essay by John Crowe Ransom: "That is simply a bad poem whose unfashionable or dated diction the plain reader spots at the first reading." But other parts of the newly-conquered territory are being little cultivated. A belated critical posse in full jungle kit still hacks its way through these no longer very forbidding areas, in the pages of the semi-academic reviews; and that is about all. The influence of the generation of 1914 was always of a peculiar kind. On taste, ideas and feelings about literature it was dynamic, radical, and in the end largely triumphant. A diluted version of Mr. Eliot's critical doctrine (and that includes, at one remove, a great deal of the doctrines of Hulme, Pound and Lewis) is by now the possession of undergraduates and schoolboys. Mr. Eliot's version of English literary history is as much an orthodoxy as Matthew Arnold's was a generation before. Yet the direct effect on literary practice has been strangely small. There is no other poem of any significance remotely like *The Waste Land;* the metrics and the ordonnance of Pound's *Propertius* have had no successors whatever; no one has ever seriously attempted to emulate Joyce's most characteristic experiments; and the extraordinary bundle of detestations that go to make up Wyndham Lewis are so arbitrary that they are a monument to nothing but himself.

A rich and vigorous body of literature has established itself, but has not established a workable tradition. A possibility (it has been faintly entertained by Mr. Blackmur)[3] is that it is not through this self-consciously "modern" literature that the main road runs; that these writers are not the transmitters of the most

7

vigorous poetic life of our time. Perhaps the authentic torch has been borne by writers of a more traditional cast—shall we say by Robert Frost, Robert Graves and E. M. Forster? But this is not really a possibility. It is not the admirable workers in traditional modes who have given the twentieth century its peculiar kind of vitality. The suggestion is entertained only to be dismissed. As I show it to the door I become aware of one of its relatives faintly demanding admittance. Deep in the folk-memory of English literary critics is the echo of a time when it was possible to speak of something called "the English spirit." Few, in a state of full vigilance, would allow this faded trope to escape their lips now. But I intend to employ it, not meaning whatever Sir Arthur Quiller-Couch would have meant by it, but meaning something like the spirit of the language, the whole drift and pressure given by the whole body of poetry written in English. The suggestion that knocks at the door is that specifically "modern" poetry is hostile to this spirit and has tried to move against that pressure. A few very powerful talents succeeded in establishing idiosyncratic positions. No one since has been powerful enough to take up the same stance or sufficiently supple and adaptable to go back and take up the old path where it left off. This is at least plausible as far as English is concerned, though in America it may be less so. It need not surprise us when we consider that two of the "men of

1914" were Americans, one an Irishman, and the origins of the other shrouded in mystery.

The suggestion may be allowed to stand in the doorway, for we are not yet in a position to examine its credentials. We have not yet asked what the nature of the twentieth-century revolution is, so we cannot yet know how it is related to the English poetic tradition. It is notable that whatever was happening in those years has not yet acquired a name. Mr. Blackmur has referred to the whole European movement, with which the English one belongs, as Expressionism. I should not be very happy with this as far as our domestic affair is concerned. Expressionism in art has Germanic connotations, and the literature we are considering is Anglo-American profoundly influenced by France. And Expressionism is a name for a kind of critical doctrine, a doctrine of personality and self-expression, that is precisely the one *not* held by our twentieth century school. I should like to have a name; it is a nuisance not to have one for something one is always discussing; but I should prefer to look nearer home and hope to fare better.

If we look into the archives of the period of revolutionary preparation, the name that is going about is Imagism. A "school of images" is referred to. Ezra Pound announces that as for the future the "Imagistes" have that in their keeping. This was in a note to the complete poetical works of T. E. Hulme (five poems), published at the end of *Ripostes* in 1912. Several forms of an Imagist manifesto exist; and Ezra Pound's "A few don'ts by an Imagist" appeared in *Poetry* in 1913. And there are several Imagist anthologies, the first under the auspices of Ezra Pound, others under those of Amy Lowell. In the narrow sense, the name refers to a movement whose history was brief, broken and querulous, whose poetic results were minuscule. The refinement of our numbers was to be accomplished by the introduction of the *haiku,* the Japanese poem of seventeen syllables. The tongue that Milton spake is not easily compressed into seventeen-syllable units; and even in its longer flights Imagism remains a small affair. But as a centre and an influence it is not small. It is the hard irreducible core of a whole cluster of poetic ideas that extend far beyond Imagism as a movement. Imagist ideas are at the centre of the characteristic poetic procedures of our time, and there is a case for giving the word a wider extension.

Imagism sounds like a by-blow from Symbolism. Image and symbol—we have been pestered by both words long enough; often we do not distinguish between them. If we were talking about continental Europe instead of the Anglo-American literary world there would be no need to make much play with Imagism. Symbolism is already there, well established and more or less understood. There have been several attempts to see the new poetry in English simply as a part of this earlier European movement. Edmund Wilson sees it in this way, as a large extension of Symbolism, in *Axel's Castle*. But this justly famous book was written in the middle of the development that it describes, and has been overtaken by the event. Its introductory chapter on Symbolism seems thin today, though it was nourishing at the time. Sir Maurice Bowra, largely concerned with Europe, has written of modern literature as the heritage of Symbolism. More recently, Frank Kermode, in a brief, brilliant, unhistorical essay, *Romantic Image,* has conflated Symbolism and Imagism, and even seen both of them as a continuation of the Romantic road. However, there is room for a distinction here, and not only room, but a real need for it.

Though Symbolism is in a sense a late development of Romantic thought it takes a decisively new turn. The great Romantic writers (Wordsworth, Coleridge, Keats) all see literature as deeply rooted in experience. The confessional poem, the truth that has been "proved upon our pulses," the attitude of those "to whom the miseries of the world are misery and will not let them rest"—these are its characteristic expressions. Symbolism moves in the direction of an autonomous art, severed from life and experience by an impassable gulf. The Symbolists share with the Romantics the reliance on the epiphany, the moment of revelation; but they differ sharply about its status in nature and its relation to art. Wordsworth's spiritual life is founded on such moments of illumination, and it is the business of his poetry both to describe them and to relate them to the whole experience of a long ordered lifetime. For the Symbolist poet there is no question of describing an experience; the moment of illumination only occurs in its embodiment in some particular artistic form. There is no question of relating it to the experience of a lifetime, for it is unique, it exists in the poem alone. Rimbaud's *alchimie du verbe* is not a mere phrase, for the poet not only transmits, he creates the revelations that make up his world.

Symbolism therefore has strong transcendental overtones. The poet is a magus, calling reality into existence. Or he is the sole transmitter of a mysterious system of correspondences that actually pervades the universe, but only becomes apparent in art. Or he is capable of evoking from the *Anima Mundi* symbols of the profoundest import, but strictly unexpoundable, for their content is inseparable from the form of their first expression. At times we seem to be in something like the medieval symbolic universe. But that symbolism has a key, a key given once and for all in revelation. Since the means of grace and some means of instruction are available to all, it was in a sense a joy in widest commonalty spread; while the Symbolist universe reveals itself only in glimpses, only in art, and only to initiates.

Imagism and Its Consequences

Now while modern literature has been afflicted with a persistent hangover from the rich Symbolist symposium, the magical and transcendental pretensions of Symbolism have almost entirely disappeared. It is only in the work of the early Yeats that we can find the Symbolist doctrine in full bloom. Even here it is considerably contaminated with a non-literary occultism —theosophy, spiritualism, Madame Blavatsky and the order of the Golden Dawn. It is doubtful whether we can properly speak of a Symbolist movement in English poetry, in a historical sense. Of course, if we like to take Symbolism as a universal, recurrent phenomenon we can rope in such diverse figures as Blake and Herman Melville, and no doubt a dozen others, and make some use of the concept. I am speaking of Symbolism as a more or less dateable historical development, as the term is used in French literature. This development several times looks as though it is going to occur in English, but it never comes to much, though relations with the French movement were frequent and beguiling. There was a foreshadowing of French Symbolism in the Pre-Raphaelites; there were many importations of Symbolist doctrine in the nineties; but it is not until the years before the first world war that French doctrines and practice showed signs of giving rise to a new poetry in England.

The history is complicated, and it has still only partly been written. There are probably many reasons that

Imagism and Its Consequences

Symbolism took such feeble roots in England. We had a little of it of our own already; English poetry lacks a Baudelaire to stand as *éminence grise* behind the movement; above all, Symbolist influence on sensibility was not paralleled by a close study of Symbolist forms. The *fin-de-siècle*, fertile in sentiments and attitudes that are important for modern literature, was curiously powerless to find forms to match them; and it was not until the years around 1910 that a radically new poetry, and that implies a new poetic form, really begins to appear in English. In those years, when the group that were later to call themselves Imagists were laying their plans, the transcendental pretensions of Symbolism were no longer easy to entertain. The career of Mallarmé had ended in silence and something like despair. *Un coup de dès jamais n'abolira le hasard.* Rimbaud's defection to slave-trading in Africa was itself a symbol of the inefficacy of magical Symbolism; and the innocuous chastities of Japanese poetry in dilute translation were focussing attention on the surface properties rather than on the mystic attributes of the symbol.

Certain aspects of Symbolist doctrine persist, but the nature of the attention is changed. Revelation becomes technique, incantation becomes a code of prohibitions. What emerges is a new phenomenon, to which we rightly give a new name—Imagism. Not to deal in definition at this stage, and in the hope that things

14

will become clearer as we go on, we can describe it roughly as Symbolism without the magic. The symbol, naked and unexplained, trailing no clouds of glory, becomes the image.

Let us clip a few flowers from the imagist's garden of maxims:

> An image is that which presents an intellectual and emotional complex in an instant of time.
>
> Go in fear of abstractions.
>
> The natural object is always the adequate symbol.
>
> I believe that the proper and perfect symbol is the natural object, that if a man uses "symbols" he must so use them that their symbolic function does not obtrude; so that *a* sense, and the poetic quality of the passage, is not lost to those who do not understand the symbol as such, to whom, for instance, a hawk is a hawk.[4]

Unexceptionable sentiments, according to the canons of much modern poetics; but compare them with some pure symbolist pronouncements:

> A symbol is indeed the only possible expression of some invisible essence, a transparent lamp about a spiritual flame.[5]
>
> Je dis: une fleur! et, hors de l'oubli où ma voix relègue aucun contour, en tant que quelque chose d'autre que les calices sus, musicalement se lève, idèe même et suave, l'absente de tous bouquets.[6]

These alone will serve to illustrate the way the symbol has become *opaque* in transforming itself into the image. No transparent envelopes, or mysterious

absences, or invisible essences. Direct treatment of the
thing, we are told, is the great object. T. E. Hulme's
early criticism hammers away at accurate description,
hardness, clarity. And we know what came of it:

> The apparition of these faces in the crowd;
> Petals on a wet, black bough.[7]

Those dozens of little poems in Pound's *Ripostes*
and later; clear, limited, without resonance, without
transparency. "The natural object is always the adequate symbol"—but of what? Of nothing but itself. A
world composed of atomic notations, each image separate from all the others. They neither lead into each
other nor to apprehension on any other level. There is
in all Pound's practice and theory at this time a posi-
tivism, a defiant insistence on the surface of things, and
an insistence that the surface of things is all.

Pound writes of Laurent Tailhade:

> I think this sort of clear presentation is of the noblest
> tradition of our craft. It is surely the scourge of fools.
> It is what may be called the "prose tradition" of
> poetry, and by this I mean that it is a practice of
> speech common to good prose and good verse alike.
> . . . It means constatation of fact. It presents. It does
> not comment. . . . It is not a criticism of life. I mean
> it does not deal in opinion. It washes its hands of
> theories. It does not attempt to justify anybody's ways
> to anybody or anything else.[8]

But even Pound could not consistently maintain that
the clear presentation of the object was the sole aim of

poetry. Though he often talks in T. E. Hulme's terms, as though presentational accuracy was an end in itself, in other places the natural object is seen as the equivalent of an emotion. Poetry is the art of making equations for emotions. But it is an equation of which one side only is to be presented. Imagist convention forbids that most ancient recipe for a poem—the poem in which first a natural object is presented, and then some reflection on human experience that arises from it, or is in some way parallel to it. As a student of Provençal Pound must have been familiar with the *reverdie* and its long history—the spring song, whose first stanza presents "the soote sesoun that bud and bloom forth brings," whose later ones present the happy love that resembles it, or the unhappy love that contrasts with it. By his subsequent lights it is only possible for the poet to say "It is Spring"—and, unspoken, on no account to be uttered, only to be understood—"if you care to make any deductions from this to my state of mind, you may." But since the natural object is always the adequate symbol the poem will not make itself responsible for any of these deductions.

> I leaned against a sturdy oak,
> I thought it was a trusty tree;
> But first it bent and syne it broke,
> Sae did my true love lichtly me.

This is too explicit for true Imagist principles. The proper procedure is to be seen in Pound's "Fan-Piece, for her Imperial Lord":

> O fan of white silk,
>   clear as the frost on the grass-blade,
> You also are laid aside.[9]

So far, merely a change of rhetorical convention; a laconic novelty of procedure that has its own charm. We know well enough what the Imagists are tired of. They are tired of Arnold's "Dover Beach"; the extended picture of the moonlight, the beach and the tide; and then the inevitable, the too-long expected "The sea of faith was once too at the full . . ."; the melancholy nineteenth-century automatism by which no natural object can appear without trailing its inglorious little cloud of moralising behind it. They were right to be tired. One aspect of the history of poetry is an intermittent warfare against automatisms, clichés of feeling and expression. Only an intermittent warfare, for there are long periods when poetry can rest, contented, healthy and active, within a set of received conventions. But these periods come to an end. This was a time when the battlefront had again become particularly active.

From this point of view Imagism was good tactics, and the skirmish was conducted with vigour and address. But tactics are not principles, and there is always danger when they are erected into principles. Pound was particularly liable to make this transformation. His insistence on procedure and technique is the beginning of this. "A few don'ts"; as though the writing of poetry is the adroit employment of a series of gimmicks; the continual invocation of "the expert"; the deference (in writing that shows little deference) to the progress of the natural sciences:

> What the expert is tired of to-day the public will be tired of to-morrow.
> It is not necessary that a poem should rely on its music, but if it does rely on its music that music must be such as will delight the expert.
> The scientist does not expect to be acclaimed as a great scientist until he has *discovered* something. He begins by learning what has been discovered already. He goes from that point onward.
> The best history of literature, more particularly of poetry, would be a twelve-volume anthology in which each poem was chosen . . . because it contained an invention, a definite contribution to the art of verbal expression.[10]

When Imagist doctrine was reinforced by Pound's study (if it can be called study) of Chinese, and his understanding (which was a misunderstanding) of the nature of Chinese ideogram, the gimmicks were well on the way to becoming a principle. When Pound took over Fenollosa's manuscripts he also took over the idea that the originally pictographic nature of the Chinese written character was still a subsistent force, that the reader actually *saw* the image in the complex ideogram. All scholars now agree that this is mistaken; even if they did not, it is on the face of it impossible; as impossible as to suppose that the reader of English resuscitates every dead metaphor as he goes along, thinks of weighing when he ponders, or of the stars when he considers. Even though it was untrue, this way of thinking might have given rise, when applied to an Indo-European language, to some sort of doctrine of radical metaphor—that poetry proceeds by distilling the quintessence of language. This, we have been told, is one of the keys to Mallarmé. But Pound shows no interest in this sort of speculation. His supposed nugget of wisdom from the East is used to provide a cultural foundation for the doctrine of the image. Chinese uses picture-writing and so ought we. A strain of crotchety hostility to the traditions of Western thinking begins to appear. An obscure ideological war is invented in which Confucius knocks out Aristotle and abstraction and discursive thought are left in ruins. Poetry proceeds by the juxtaposition of ideograms, and new ideogram is old image writ large. The unit of poetry is the pictograph, the record of a significant glimpse.

From then on the doctrine burgeons, flourishes, spreads its roots and sends up suckers in every direction. (Many of us have been suckers for it at one time or another.) It connects itself easily with other speculations and manoeuvres which start from a different point but begin to converge with Imagism. Joyce's "epiphany," the moment in which the essential nature of an object reveals itself, is presented with a good deal

of Thomistic top-dressing; but it is really a survival
from magical Symbolism, and our sense of this is con-
firmed by the *fin-de-siècle* prose in which the earlier
Joycean epiphanies are often enshrined. The moment
of revelation need not be a revelation of beauty or
transcendence. The customs-house clock, Stephen tells
Cranly, might suddenly be epiphanised—manifest itself
in its essence.[11] Or more frequently, a quotidian object
suddenly reveals not only its own nature, but that of
the forces that went to make it, or of the whole
circumambient situation: "one of those brown brick
houses which seem the very incarnation of Irish paraly-
sis." This can become something like a form of Imagist doctrine; more sophisticated, without the pinched
prohibitory air that hangs round Imagism. It produces
similar technical results—the instantaneous glimpse of
a phenomenal object as the basic symbolic counter.
Portrait of the Artist is built out of a succession of
such instants. Compared with the startling technical
innovations of Joyce's later work its method is unsur-
prising. It is nevertheless one of the earliest examples
of a narrative, a development, presented by a series
of unlinked scenes or shots.

One of the most celebrated offshoots of the Imagist
idea is Mr. Eliot's Objective Correlative. We are all
heartily sick of the phrase, even Mr. Eliot, so I will
only recall briefly its original formulation. "The only
way of expressing emotion in the form of art is by

finding an 'objective correlative'; in other words, a set of objects, a situation, a chain of events which shall be the formula of that *particular* emotion; such that when the external facts, which must terminate in sensory experience, are given, the emotion is immediately evoked."[12] Objections have been made to the "expressionist" character of this passage—the suggestion that the business of the poet is to find external manifestations for previously determinate emotions. I wish to point to something rather different—the suggestion that the whole natural world offers to the poet a collection of bric-à-brac from which he takes selections to represent emotional states. "Direct presentation of the thing"—the image so produced exists to be one side of an equation the other side of which is an emotion. Plainly an eccentric view of the poet's procedure. We can hardly suppose that either the author of the *Iliad* or the author of

> Christ, that my love was in my arms
> And I in my bed again

were collecting *objets trouvés* in this way. Gerard Manley Hopkins wrote "The Wreck of the Deutschland" because he was moved by the account of a shipwreck in which five nuns were drowned; he did not go round looking for a suitable disaster to match an emotion that he already had. This is possibly a position that Mr. Eliot, who wrote of it a long time ago, would not wish to maintain in its full rigour. But we

22

must in some sense hold him to it, for it has consequences in other parts of his thinking about poetry. There is the idea that coherence and validity of thought have nothing to do with poetic worth; Dante made great poetry out of a strong and beautiful philosophy, Shakespeare out of a muddled one, but this does not affect their merit as poets. There is the related idea that poets do not "think," they take over the thought of their time. This would make the poet's activity something like painting flowers on china plates that he had bought ready-made from the factory; and I am sure that this is not what Mr. Eliot means; but it is what he appears to be saying. There is the idea that meaning is a kind of sop thrown to the intellect, like the bit of meat the burglar keeps to give to the dog, while the "poetry" does its work.[13] These are all pervasive ideas in modern, post-symbolist poetic strategy, and they are all related to the root idea that the substance of poetry is the image and its resonances.

The doctrine has its corollary when we come to consider the major structure of poetry; one that is startlingly at variance with the classical view. If poetry is a matching up of images with emotions its underlying framework consists of emotions. Its order is therefore an order of emotions. In classical poetic theory (by classical I mean here one that prevailed generally from the Greeks till some time in the nineteenth century) the order of poetry was an order of events or thoughts. Events are capable of causal connection, thoughts of logical connection; the one is the structure of narrative or dramatic poetry, the other of philosophic or reflective poetry. Only in the briefest lyric can we find an order that is simply that of emotions; and classical poetic theory was not deduced from brief lyrics. One does not insist on an Aristotelian rigour of construction; but even in the looser forms the sense of a syntax of events or a syntax of thoughts is preserved; and criticism insisted on it. Emotions are not capable of such a syntax. A pattern can be made of them, by simple juxtaposition, but it will hardly be an integrated pattern, unless there runs through it the thread of narrative or logic. Imagist poetry has therefore been obliged to invoke *another kind of logic,* a logic of emotions that works in its own way, and is supposed to be especially suitable for poetry. The most compendious expression of this notion is to be found in Mr. Eliot's introduction to St. John Perse's *Anabase:*

> . . . any obscurity of the poem, on first readings, is due to the suppression of 'links in the chain,' of explanatory and connecting matter, and not to incoherence, or to the love of cryptogram. The justification of such abbreviation of method is that the sequence of images coincides and concentrates into one intense impression of barbaric civilisation. The reader has to allow the images to fall into his memory successively without questioning the reasonableness of each at the moment; so that, at the end, a total effect is produced.
>
> Such selection of a sequence of images and ideas has nothing chaotic about it. There is a logic of the imagi-

nation as well as a logic of concepts. People who do not appreciate poetry always find it difficult to distinguish between order and chaos in the arrangement of images; and even those who are capable of appreciating poetry cannot depend upon first impressions. I was not convinced of Mr. Perse's imaginative order until I had read the poem five or six times. And if, as I suggest, such an arrangement of imagery requires just as much 'fundamental brainwork' as the arrangement of an argument, it is to be expected that the reader of a poem should take at least as much trouble as a barrister reading an important decision on a complicated case.[14]

This document is worth examining in some detail. The occasion is particular, but the application is general. What is outlined is the method of a school. Three layers are to be discerned in this ingenious piece of discourse. The first is simply descriptive. We are told of a "sequence of images," of images that fall into the memory successively with no question of reasonableness, of resultant obscurity. This is a general description of Imagist technique; it is the procedure of *Anabase;* it is also the procedure of *The Waste Land* and the *Cantos.* The second layer, interwoven with the first, but we are attempting to separate it, is one of justification. Two justifications of this method are in fact offered. They are not compatible with each other. The first is that any appearance of obscurity is merely due to the suppression of connecting matter: the logic of the poem is like the logic of any other kind of discourse, but it is presented in a concentrated and elliptical form. The second justification, however, is that the poem is constructed according to a "logic of the imagination" which is different from ordinary logic. It requires as much effort as the construction of an argument, but it is evidently of a different kind. And besides these layers, of description and justification, there is a third layer of knock-me-down *argumentum ad hominem,* designed to cause alarm and despondency in the breasts of persons who have not yet accepted the first two. Such persons do not appreciate poetry, cannot distinguish between order and chaos, and, in their benighted triviality, have probably never thought of assimilating the action of a reader of poetry to that of a barrister getting up a brief.

There is much in this sort of argument that arouses suspicion. The device of dismissing one's opponents as unqualified instead of convincing them that they are wrong is one that works only with the very unsophisticated or the very easily scared. It has been greatly overworked by the founding fathers of modern poetics. Only poets can judge poetry; this is a matter for the expert; certificates of culture countersigned by Confucius, Lancelot Andrews and Rémy de Gourmont to be produced on admission—but these minatory gestures have dwindled into a curious historic ritual; and they have been discussed elsewhere. A more serious question is whether the Imagist procedure here described is an ordinary mode of discourse telescoped and abbreviated, or whether some special "logic of the imagination" is involved.

Let us look at the organisation of *The Waste Land*. In detail, and in some places, the first explanation works well enough. The twenty opening lines of the poem can be seen as an elliptical narrative, with fragments of reflection and direct speech. ("April is the cruellest month. . . . [we] went on in sunlight, into the Hofgarten. . . . And when we were children, staying at the arch-duke's.") In principle it could be expanded, the links could be supplied; what we have is the natural result of the attempt at pruning and concentrating nineteenth-century poetic method. The sense of an existing but not definitely stated plot is still there. It will require a great deal more latitude to apply this argument to the major structure of the poem. We know now that it was of considerably greater length, and attained its present proportions under the direction of Ezra Pound. We have always known that "Death by Water," the Phlebas the Phoenician section, was not originally part of *The Waste Land,* since it is a translation from the French of the last section of an earlier poem "Dans le Restaurant." Its insertion was again due to Pound. We know too that "Gerontion" was at one time to be included but was in the end left out to become a separate poem.[15] If this is the logic of the imagination it is evidently patient of a good deal of outside influence. There is a curious fortuitousness about it. And mere ellipsis, the omission of connecting links, will not serve as an explanation of the changes of speaker, shifts in time, scene and mode of address, the liberation of the image from all continuity that give the poem its peculiarly coruscating surface. In the poem as a whole the sense of an unspoken underlying plot has completely disappeared.

I cannot think that the problems raised by the structure of *The Waste Land* have been faced. They have been a party matter, a matter for polemic or defence; they have been a shibboleth; to accept this sort of technique was at one time a sort of touchstone for participation in modern poetry. Above all, the methodological anfractuosities of the piece have fulfilled one of the main economic functions of poetry in this century —they have given employment to a host of scholiasts. But they have hardly been a matter for disinterested enquiry. While the poem was still capable of causing bewilderment it established itself. The brilliance of the imagery, the auditory and incantatory grandeur of its best passages, stole into the consciousness and became a part of our poetical property; it became ungrateful, almost indecent to ask of what sort of continuum these fragments were a part. And we became satisfied with a level of coherence that we should never have found sufficient in any earlier poem. The unity of emotional effect withdrew attention from the logical discontinuity, the extraordinary rhetorical diversity. A poem about frustration, aridity, fear and the perversions of love—these signs were to be read by anyone. They were read, and in combination with the modern urban imagery they instigated the critics who said that the poem expressed "the disillusionment of a generation." For this, some years later, they were sternly reproved by the author; but they were no doubt expressing, in their way, the only sense they had of a unity of purpose in the poem. Meanwhile, prompted by the notes, many persons who had stopped reading *The Golden Bough* looked at it again, and those who had never heard of Miss Jessie Weston read *From Ritual to Romance.* None of them were bold enough to say in public that these studies did little to advance their understanding. Certainly they directed attention to recurring symbolism of death and rebirth, drought and rain. But this was the kind of pattern that in earlier poetry had been only secondary to structure of another kind; it could not be seen as constituting a structure in itself. So we turned to more peripheral matters. We looked up the quotations from Dante and Baudelaire, and our apprehension of isolated lines increased in depth. *Turdus aonalaschkae pallasii,* whose water-dripping song is justly celebrated, doubtless afforded satisfaction to many. And the volume of exegesis increased, the explanations that did not explain, the links that connected nothing to nothing.

And by the time that the movement of modern poetry had gone far enough for it to be a possible object of contemplation and enquiry, one shrank from asking the real questions, lest what was after all one of the great poetic experiences of our time should be still further buried beneath yet another load of waste paper.

But the questions remain—above all the question of what really makes the poem a totality, if it is one at all. If we can imagine some ideal critic, acquainted with the poetical tradition of Europe, yet innocent of the spirit of our age, and if we can imagine ourselves persuading him to leave the question of total structure in abeyance, "to allow the images to fall into his memory successively without questioning the reasonableness of each"—he would still be struck by the extraordinary rhetorical incongruities. He would find within its four hundred lines passages that are narrative, others that are dramatic, descriptive, lyric, hallucinatory and allusive. The theory of genres was never watertight or exhaustive, but never before was there a poem of this length, or perhaps of any other length, in which the modes were so mixed. Nor is the rhetorical level any more constant than the rhetorical mode. A modern and highly individual elegiac intensity, pastiche Renaissance grandeur, sharp antithetical social comment in the Augustan manner, the low mimetic of public house conversation—all these and probably several other styles are found side by side. The relation

of these is sometimes obvious; it is one of calculated
contrast. But it is a question how hard such contrasts
of texture can be worked in a relatively short poem
without disastrous damage to the unity of surface.
It is not so much in the obvious collisions of the high
and the low styles that this is felt. That kind of calculated shock action is a limited effect, and the intention of producing the shock itself provides a medium
between the two elements. It is the use of language in
different and unrelated fashions in different parts of the
poem that is disruptive. There is the lovely, roman-
tically evocative manner of the hyacinth girl passage:

> Yet when we came back, late, from the Hyacinth garden,
> Your arms full, and your hair wet, I could not
> Speak, and my eyes failed, I was neither
> Living nor dead, and I knew nothing,
> Looking into the heart of light, the silence.

These lines live unhappily in the same poem with:

> Endeavours to engage her in caresses
> Which still are unreproved, if undesired.
> Flushed and decided, he assaults at once;
> Exploring hands encounter no defence;
> His vanity requires no response,
> And makes a welcome of indifference.

The uneasiness does not arise from incompatibility
of tone and feeling, but because the two passages are
using language in utterly different ways; the first to
evoke, by overtones and connotations, the trembling
ghost of an intense emotion that is never located or

defined; the second to define a situation by precise denotation and intelligent analysis. It is as though a painter were to employ a pointilliste technique in one part of a picture, and the glazes of the high renaissance in another.

When we come to the content of the separate passages the situation is disturbing in another way. It has become fashionable to refer to these contents as "themes," suggesting a vaguely musical analogy; and suggesting, too, I suppose, that the "themes" of a poem are related to each other only as the themes of a musical composition are. But themes in a poem are made of words, and words have meanings; our attention is never arrested at the verbal surface; it proceeds to what the words denote. They denote objects, persons and ideas; and it is very difficult altogether to dispel the notion that the objects, persons and ideas in a single poem should be in some intelligible relation to one another. A very little inspection of the commentaries, or questioning of readers of the poem, will show that this is not the case with *The Waste Land;* there is no certainty either about what is denoted, or how it is related to other denotations. It is sometimes suggested, for example, that the hyacinth girl is or might be the same as the lady who stayed with her cousin the archduke a few lines earlier. To me it has always been obvious that these fragmentary glimpses showed us, and were designed to show us, two different kinds of

women and two different kinds of human relationship. I suppose that those who think otherwise have
taken at least as much trouble and are no greater fools
than I. And I see no means by which the matter could
be decided.

We have already remarked that Phlebas the Phoenician had a prior existence in another context and
was included by chance or outside suggestion. True, a
place is rather arbitrarily prepared for him; Madame
Sosostris the clairvoyant, who is supposed to be using
a Tarot pack, produces the card of the drowned Phoenician sailor—which is not a member of the Tarot
pack—in order to suggest in advance that Phlebas has
some part in the structure of the poem. But what his
part is remains quite uncertain. Here the commenta-
tors for the most part insist on resolutely marking
time, for fear of committing themselves to a false step;
and we are even bidden to observe that the "currents"
which pick the drowned Phlebas's bones have a fore-
runner in the "currants" in the pocket of Mr. Euge-
nides the Smyrna merchant. Surely the last refuge of
baffled imbecility.

It has been said that the poem adopts a "stream of
consciousness" technique;[16] and this sounds reassuring
without committing us to anything very much. But it
is precisely what the poem does not do. The advantage
of the "stream of consciousness" technique is that it
allows a flood of images, more or less emancipated

from narrative or logical continuity, while still preserving a psychological continuity—the continuity of
inhering in a single consciousness. *The Waste Land*
conspicuously foregoes this kind of unifying principle.
One desperate expedient has been to fasten on Mr.
Eliot's note to line 218: "Tiresias, although a mere
spectator and not indeed a 'character,' is yet the most
important personage in the poem, uniting all the rest.
. . . What Tiresias *sees,* in fact, is the substance of the
poem." In the light of this it can be suggested that the
whole poem is Tiresias's "stream of consciousness."[17]
This is probably to give the note more weight than it
can bear, and in any case, it does little to the purpose.
Who was Tiresias? A man who had also been a woman,
who lived forever and could foretell the future. That
is to say, not a single human consciousness, but a
mythological catch-all, and as a unifying factor of no
effect whatever.

I should like to commit myself to the view that for
a poem to exist as a unity more than merely bibliog-
raphical, we need the sense of one voice speaking, as
in lyric or elegiac verse; or of several voices intelligibly
related to each other, as in narrative with dialogue or
drama; that what these voices say needs a principle of
connection no different from that which would be
acceptable in any other kind of discourse; that the
collocation of images is not a method at all, but the
negation of method. In fact, to expose oneself com-

pletely, I want to say that a poem, internally considered, ought to make the same kind of sense as any other discourse.

This should amount to a frontal attack on the main positions of modern poetics. I cannot feel that I have the equipment for this enterprise, nor if I had that it would be the right way to proceed. If the conviction I have baldly stated is just, its justice will be seen, in due time, not by virtue of a puny attack from a single criticaster, but by what Johnson calls the common sense of readers uncorrupted by literary prejudice. So I only wish to press my point in two directions of which I feel fairly certain, neither of them quite central.

For the first I return to the sentence of Johnson I have just quoted. "By the common sense of readers uncorrupted with literary prejudices, after all the refinements of subtlety and the dogmatism of learning, must be finally decided all claim to poetical honours." These are words that no one who cares about poetry in our century can read without a twinge. The appeal to a body of readers who are not specialists or eccentrics, who are merely representative of the common sentiment and intelligence of human kind, is one we feel ourselves so little able to make, one that we know so well, if we are honest, ought to be made— that we can think of it only with a feeling of distress. Where is contemporary poetry read, and where is it written? In the universities. Who reads it? Students;

professional students of literature mostly, and professors, who expect to write papers on it, or to lecture on it—to "explicate" it, in the current technical cant. What has become (not to go back to some pre-lapsarian Eden) of the kind of public that even so recent a poet as Tennyson could enjoy? It has been warned off; it has been treated to sneers, threats and enigmas. It has been told so often that it has no status and no business in the sacred wood, and it has found the business actually being transacted there so remote from its ordinary apprehension, that it has turned away, in indifference, or disgust, or despair. A complex of social reasons is often produced to account for this; no doubt some of them are valid. A covert notion of social determinism is invoked to produce a sensation of comforting hopelessness about almost any undesirable situation today. But that is not my business. I am only concerned with what is intrinsic to poetry; and much of the reason for the narrow appeal of modern poetry is in the poetry itself. The wilful Alexandrianism, the allusiveness and multiplicity of reference, above all, the deliberate cultivation of modes of organisation that are utterly at variance with those of ordinary discourse—these are the main reasons for the disappearance of Johnson's common reader. It is hard to say this, for to say it lines one up with the hostile, the malicious and the Philistine, with all those who hate and suspect the exploring sensibility and have never made the attempt to penetrate into the imaginative life of their time. But it is sometimes necessary to risk being put in bad company for the sake of saying what seems to be true. One can only hope that one has better reasons for saying it.

For my second point I hope to produce a better reason. The poem that abandons the syntax of narrative or argument and relies on the interplay of "themes" or the juxtaposition of images according to the mysterious laws of poetic logic is not, so far as it is doing anything positive at all, doing anything that poetry has not done before. Clustered and repeated images, contrasts or echoes among them, a half-heard music of this kind has always been part of poetic effect. We have always partly known it, and modern criticism has done much to make it explicit. But in all poetry before our time this music has been background music. What we have heard with the alert and directed attention has been something different. It has been a story, or an argument, or a meditation, or the direct expression of feeling. Modern criticism has aroused our sense of this second sub-rational layer in our appreciation of poetry. Perhaps the most signal instance of this is the Shakespeare criticism of Wilson Knight, which sees the plays not as patterns made by character in action, but as "expanded metaphors," patterns of "themes" and "images." Modern poetry in the Imagist mode has performed the extraordinary manoeuvre of shifting its whole weight to this second level. It has shorn itself of paraphrasable sense, of all narrative or discursive line, and relies on the play of contrasted images alone. In doing so it has achieved a startling concentration and brilliance of the individual image, and a whole new rhetoric of its own, with its own special kind of fascination. I still wish to maintain that it is an inadequate rhetoric, inadequate for anything but very short poems and very special effects—states of madness and dream, for example. I take it that the case of Pound's *Cantos* goes without saying; they are the wreckage of poetry; brilliant passages, sometimes long, sometimes the merest splinters, floating in a turbid sea of stammering and incoherent mumble. But even in *The Waste Land* and the *Four Quartets,* where the level of the individual passages is far more consistent, and where it is just possible to give their arrangement some sort of publicly valid justification, the organising principle is still quite inadequate for poems of this scope. These poems survive, and will survive, not assisted by their structure, but in spite of it.

This is true of much of the work of Pound, Eliot and Wallace Stevens—to name three of the founding fathers of modern poetry. Their poetry suffers, even on the level on which it functions so persuasively and brilliantly, from the lack of any other level, the lack of public, explicit, paraphrasable discourse. We know, of course, about the "heresy of paraphrase" as it has been called—that we ought never to suppose that a paraphrase can tell us what a poem is "about." Perhaps we ought never to paraphrase a poem; but as with many other things that we ought never to do, we ought also to be able to feel that we could do it. The virtue that we exercise in not making a conceptual prose translation of a modern poem is generally a fugitive and cloistered virtue; for it would not be possible to give any such translation if we tried. To attempt to explain to an intelligent person who knows nothing about twentieth-century poetry how *The Waste Land* works is to be overcome with embarrassment at having to justify principles so affected, so perverse, so deliberately removed from the ordinary modes of rational communication. If poetry were to go on in this way it would develop before long into an esoteric entertainment with as much relevance to the experience of the common reader as, say, heraldry or real tennis. The imagist revolution was a sort of spring-cleaning; a much-needed spring-cleaning that got rid of a great deal of the fusty, obstructive and dust-gathering matter that had cluttered up the weaker poetry of the nineteenth century. But the house has not been comfortable to live in ever since. And the clotted rubbish of academic imagist criticism is already beginning to fill it up again. There is no reason to be optimistic about this situation. Poetry can degenerate into a meaningless esoteric exercise, and go on that way for centuries. It has happened. But perhaps it will not happen to us. And we have the example of the greatest poet of the early twentieth century to show that it need not. It is something of a paradox that Yeats, whose beliefs are often supposed to be more fantastic and irrational than those of any other great mind of our time, should never have lost his faith in rational order and the disposing intelligence as the guiding principle of a poem.

II.

Imagist Poetry
and the Tradition

About forty years ago it was possible to be deeply
engaged with literature, as a writer or a student, yet
to be entirely innocent of any concern with literary
theory. This is hardly possible now. One of the minor
accompaniments of the Imagist revolution has been,
as everybody knows, an immense elaboration of critical thinking. The man of letters (if the word has still
any meaning today) is almost obliged to have explicit
opinions about matters that his predecessors were content to leave to professional aestheticians. This might
have led to a general enlightenment and a more general
consensus of literary opinion, but a very little examination of current critical journals will show that it has
not. No doubt the prophets and the patriarchs, by the
time they reached the age of fifty and surveyed the
intellectual life of their time, were apt to say that they
did not know what the world was coming to; and
this precedent has been generally followed ever since;
but the sense of uncertainty in judging immediately
contemporary literature can hardly ever have been
greater than it is today; and in current judgments on
the work of the past the picture is not much clearer.

There is a babel of confused noise; some of it is just the busy hum of academics taking in each other's washing; but some of it arises from quite fundamental disagreement. Wire-drawn discussions, often far removed from the concrete realities of poetic experience, invite an easy scepticism: but debate about what literature is, what it does, about the status of our imaginative experience and its relation to our past history, cannot be unimportant. We can look back with mild regret to a time when such matters were largely settled by custom and unspoken agreement, but this is not our situation. Once a bundle of experiences has been made the subject of open disputation, there is nothing to do but have it out—unless of course we prefer to pull our coats about our ears and wait till history has it out for us.

A degree of confusion in these matters is not of course unfamiliar. Literary theory has never from the beginning been an orderly affair, with a regular dialectic. Contradictions have been frequent, and mere failures to connect have been more frequent. We should expect judgments of value to differ from one age to another; but they sometimes agree, on quite irreconcileable grounds. Johnson would have been deeply shocked by Wordsworth's poetry, and Wordsworth was entirely hostile to the poetry and principles represented by Johnson; but they both attack Gray's odes for pretty much the same reasons. We might expect a certain agreement in judgments of fact; but we do not find it. Johnson praises Shakespeare because his characters are not individuals but species; and the Romantic critics praise him because each of his characters is so clearly individualised. And so on. It is the business of the historian of literary ideas to explain and disentangle these disorders.

Where, however, he may expect to find a fair community of thought is in the critical theory of a single period or a single school. Neo-classic criticism has its limitations, but it accounts for most of the features of neo-classic poetry, and gives us some means of seeing it in relation to the poetry of earlier times. Wordsworth's theory of poetic language has many loose ends; he does not always succeed in saying what he means, and Coleridge had to tidy it all up for him; but after all we know what Wordsworth was driving at, and we can see that the massive movement of his poetry is in roughly the same direction. Both neo-classic and Romantic poetic theory could stand a good deal of contradictory detail and imperfect formulation — for each had a philosophy and the movement of a society behind it; the large stream manages to carry the diverse elements along. The remarkable body of critical writing and literary propaganda that accompanied the rise of Imagist poetry does not seem to have the same directing energy. Bating all the possible quibbles about detail, one looks for the underlying consistency, the broad movement of a considerable stream of thought. But it is not there. Imagist poetic theory was inconsistent with itself, and large parts of it were contradicted by the contemporary poetic practice. There could hardly be a better example than the criticism of T. E. Hulme, which makes propaganda for a "hard," "dry" classical art, with weapons taken largely from romantic critics; unless it is the early criticism of Mr. Eliot, which is equally an exaltation of the classic virtues—while he was contemporaneously writing quite revolutionary poetry, of a kind that had deliberately abandoned the prime classical aims and in fact represents the extreme limits of romantic method. But there are other competitors: Ezra Pound recommending the study of traditional Romance versification as a corrective to the laxities of the age, while himself writing in a very refined late-Victorian style; and a little later evolving a brilliant and novel verse founded on Symbolist *vers libre* and the rhythms of prose. And there is Joyce, primly invoking the firm categories of St. Thomas to justify illuminations expressed in the faint wavering rhythms of Pater and the *fin-de-siècle;* Wyndham Lewis upholding the virtues of clarity and order in polemical works that are confused brilliant and explosive packages of insight, prejudice and half-digested philosophy. It is the same story in every case; enormous talent, rising at times to genius of all but the very highest order; heavily armed and brilliantly con-

ducted attacks, dashing sallies, prodigious personal
feats, capable of giving more exhilaration, more sheer
intellectual delight, than any body of criticism we
have known; but no sense of direction; none of that
sense of a deeply felt, all-organising human purpose
that we cannot fail to notice in the work of the
Romantic critics, or even in the earlier literary establishment of Dryden and Pope and Johnson.

Mr. Bateson has referred to this period as "a short
reign of terror"[1] which was necessary to discredit once
and for all the watery dregs of late nineteenth-century
aesthetics, the literary ethos represented by Watts-
Dunton, Gosse and Stopford Brooke. Ezra Pound, in a
note on T. E. Hulme, concludes that "the bleak and
smeary 'Twenties' wretchedly needed his guidance, and
the pity is that he was not there in person to keep
down vermin."[2] A reign of terror, keeping down vermin; both phrases suggest a movement clearer about
what it was against than about what it was for.
Nobody can read the early critical work of Pound and
Eliot without realising that they were against sin. It
is much less easy to see what particular virtues they
were recommending. In *The Sacred Wood* Mr. Eliot
is plainly against "The poetical vagaries of the present
age"; he is against literary impressionism; he is against
Gilbert Murray's "vulgar debasement of the eminently
personal idiom of Swinburne"; against Pater, and the
assimilation of poetry to religion. He is against, in

short, the late phase of Romanticism in which he finds himself—against Romanticism in general; "there may be a good deal to be said for Romanticism in life, there is no place for it in letters." But the quality of what we presume to be the classicism that is to take its place is extraordinarily hard to discern. Mr. Eliot at this stage approves of the destructive criticism of Arnold, approves of Aristotle and Dr. Johnson; and this sounds like a decorous English neo-classicism of a familiar kind. Yet the presiding critical influence is that of Rémy de Gourmont—acknowledged, and even if it were not acknowledged it might be suspected—a Symbolist critic of extraordinarily diverse activities and opinions, none of which could be got into the neo-classical box. It is from him that the critical ideal of *The Sacred Wood* is derived, "ériger en lois ses impressions personelles": an admirable and courageous critical ideal, which Mr. Eliot's own best critical work nobly exemplifies—but not a neo-classical one. In fact the neo-classic ideal is precisely the converse of this —to conform one's personal impressions to laws that are conceived of as pre-existing, as part of the natural order. Such positive critical unity as *The Sacred Wood* has is given by a taste—the exquisite personal taste which has always led Mr. Eliot to quote and exemplify so aptly, and thereby to become the most influential critic of his generation. But the taste can cover a multitude of uncertainties—about the relation of personality to the work of art, about the way emotions are expressed in literature, about the relation of poetry to philosophy—all of them matters of importance.

It may be suspected that these uncertainties of direction in early modern criticism are the result of a fundamental spiritual confusion, which we cannot hope to identify clearly, but might be able vaguely to locate. It is in some such area that the criticism of T. E. Hulme seems to originate. I do not want to enter into the question of how great Hulme's personal influence on his contemporaries actually was. Pound tends to play it down, and Eliot had no personal contact with him. But Hulme's ideas, either in his own formulation, or in some diffusion, or by pointing back to Hulme's own sources, or to analogues elsewhere, are fundamental to the criticism of this time; and the brash confidence with which he exposes them makes his work a particularly convenient field for inspection.

The celebrated essay "Romanticism and Classicism"[3] is both typical and central. Words fail me to record the number of fallacies and contradictions in these twenty pages; or rather, any reasonable number of words fail; it could be done at inordinate length. But the central notion is plain. It is the same idea that was made familiar a little later (Hulme's essay was written about 1914) by Irving Babbit's *Rousseau and Romanticism* (1917)—that Romanticism has a single root, the Rousseauist doctrine "that man was by nature good, that it was only bad laws and customs that had suppressed him." Hulme identifies himself with the opposite; with what he calls the classical point of view, which accepts the finite and limited nature of man; and this, he says, is also the religious view.

> Here is the root of all romanticism: that man, the individual, is an infinite reservoir of possibilities. . . . One can define the classical quite clearly as the exact opposite to this. Man is an extraordinarily fixed and limited animal whose nature is absolutely constant. It is only by tradition and organisation that anything decent can be got out of him. . . . It would be a mistake to identify the classical view with that of materialism. On the contrary it is identical with the normal religious attitude.

The essential of the religious attitude for Hulme is what he calls the same classical dogma of original sin; and this is the essential of the classical attitude too. I will not pause to wonder at the strange realignment of forces that this alliance of classicism with Christian dogma brought about, though anyone who was following these matters in the twenties will remember it as bewildering. I have only two points to make; one is the extraordinary impoverishment of the religious attitude that would follow from Hulme's formulation; the other is concerned with the literary consequences that he draws from it.

It is not worth wasting much time on Hulme's religious attitude. "Man is an extraordinarily fixed and limited animal whose nature is absolutely constant."

"Extraordinarily" can only mean "more than is ordinary with animals." Man is more fixed and limited than the lion or the horse or the duck-billed platypus? This is surely nonsense both culturally and biologically. "It is only by tradition and organisation that anything decent can be got out of him"; and this represents the religious attitude? But all the higher religions have come with the promise of bringing man deliverance from the law. It was not Rousseau, it was the Psalmist who said *Emitte spiritum tuum et creabuntur: et renovabis faciem terrae.* It was not Rousseau, it was St. Paul who spoke of Abraham "who against hope believed in hope, that he might become the father of many nations according to that which was spoken. . . . He staggered not at the promise of God through unbelief, but was strong in faith, giving glory to God; and being fully persuaded that what he had promised he was able to perform." And it was not Rousseau who was the witness of the Apocalypse. If religion were a contemplation of the natural world as a closed order—if, that is to say, faith and hope were omitted—Hulme's account of it would be true. But why go on? Anti-Rousseauism may have been a needed tonic, but when it is used to reduce religion to a depressed cosmic Toryism the limited efficacy of this nostrum becomes apparent.

And of course Hulme gives the game away himself. He is not at heart concerned with religion. His version of original sin is a political doctrine, and his performance is a projection of political doctrine into the religious sphere. One cannot accuse him of lacking candour. The names he invokes in the early paragraphs of his essay are those of "Maurras, Laserre and all the group connected with *L'Action Française.*" It is they, he says, who have made romanticism and classicism into political catchwords. It is they whose main use for classicism was as a stick to beat the Revolution. As he accurately remarked, the distinction had become a party symbol. "If you asked a man of a certain set whether he preferred the classics or the romantics, you could deduce from that what his politics were." And, though Hulme does not mention this, it was of course Maurras and the *Action Française* group who did notoriously and openly what many have been willing to do covertly—used Catholic Christendom in a purely political sense, were willing to employ Christianity simply as a right-wing political weapon. If Hulme's notion of the religious attitude came to him from this source it is not surprising that it should be an eccentric one.

The literary deductions from this are still more eccentric. Hulme foresees the arrival of a "classical" period in poetry; and this is apparently a straightforward piece of historical prognostication, such as men of letters with their ears to the ground are often liable to make. What are the qualities that the classic-religious attitude will produce in poetry? Since man is a limited creature his verse must also be limited in its aims. The literary vice of romanticism was a continual attempt at commerce with the infinite. This deplorable traffic will now cease. Ruskin wrote, "Those who have so pierced and seen the melancholy deeps of things are filled with intense passion and gentleness and sympathy." But when he did so he was thinking in the corrupt Romantic mode. For the new classical poetry "it is essential to prove that beauty may be in small, dry things": and "the particular poetry we are going to get will be cheerful, dry and sophisticated." Now in the course of developing this argument Hulme, who writes with great liveliness, if not without vulgarity, scores many effective literary hits. And his Imagist propaganda is of great interest from another point of view. But the main drift of his argument is a foolish paradox. The essential of the religious attitude is the dogma of original sin, and this is the essential of the classical attitude too. It is about to become influential again and will produce a kind of verse that is small, dry, cheerful and sophisticated. This is the natural consequence of the religious attitude, which has nothing to do with the infinite—and, I suppose we might add, has produced in the past such small, dry, cheerful and sophisticated works as the *Aeneid, Dies Irae,* the *Paradiso, Piers Plowman* and *Phèdre.* The examples are mine, but they will be enough, I imagine, to indicate the abyss of nonsense into which Hulme would lead us, by a skillful manipulation of half-truths; and into which he did lead a good many literary theorists of the generation succeeding his own.

Now all these operations of Hulme's are conducted in the name of tradition; and tradition, the word and the idea, was to become a spell to conjure with in the coming literary upheaval. What we can learn from Hulme's essay is how anomalous, how eccentric, the relation to tradition is. A fragmentary version of the Christian religious tradition is seized on. It is equated with a partial notion of classicism derived from a group of politically minded Frenchmen. (There is no indication that Hulme has thought about ancient classical literature at all, and if he had cared to look at English classicism he would surely have had to relate it to Deism rather than to traditional Christianity.) And from this mish-mash is drawn a set of literary deductions which are both logically uncompelling and historically false. When we consider the influence that ideas of this sort had, we may suspect that an eccentric and anomalous idea of tradition is generally at work. And this is what we must now try to examine.

Mr. Eliot's essay "Tradition and the Individual Talent" in *The Sacred Wood* is rightly regarded as one of the great critical documents of our time. One part of it contains the most fruitful and, I suspect, the most enduring of all suggestions towards a revised critical neo-classicism—a form of neo-classicism that is workable in the modern literary situation. To think of the existing monuments of literature as forming an ideal order, which is altered, if ever so slightly, by the addition of a really new work to the series; to demand that the new work shall both cohere with the past and alter that to which it coheres—this suggestion both satisfies our sense of an established order and makes novelty possible, as older neo-classicism did not; and it goes far to reconcile historical with aesthetic judgments. If we had to choose a single one of Mr. Eliot's critical principles to preserve and carry away with us, it would be this. But the idea of literary tradition advanced in the essay as a whole arouses doubts and questions. I believe that it suggests a wrong notion of how tradition lives and communicates itself.

The early part of the essay expounds the thesis that not only the best, but the most individual parts of a poet's work may be those parts "where the dead poets, his ancestors, assert their immortality most vigorously." The kind of continuing excellence which constitutes poetic tradition cannot be inherited; it can only be obtained by great labour. It involves the historical sense, and "the historical sense involves a perception, not only of the pastness of the past, but also of its presence; the historical sense compels a man to write not merely with his own generation in his bones, but with a feeling that the literature of Europe from

Homer and within it the whole of the literature of his
own country has a simultaneous existence and com-
poses a simultaneous order." We see why Mr. Eliot
speaks of great labour. Clearly the historical sense
involves a great deal of historical knowledge. A little
later Mr. Eliot anticipates the objection that this seems
to require a ridiculous amount of erudition, and that
any such demand is contradicted by the educations and
careers of many poets in all ages. But he does not really
answer it. He suggests that the genius of a special kind
can acquire his history by a sort of osmosis, from a very
few or very accidental sources; but this is not what he
was saying before; it is a contradiction of the plain
sense that his earlier words must bear.

For he has already told us that the poet cannot "take
the past as a lump, an indiscriminate bolus, nor can
he form himself wholly upon one or two private
admirations, nor can he form himself wholly upon one
preferred period." He must be aware of the mind of
Europe, and of the mind of his own country, and be
aware that it is much more important than his private
mind. An honourable programme, but one reflects that
the mind of Europe is a very extensive object of awareness. It includes the Encyclopedists as well as the Fathers of the Church, Spinoza as well as St. Bernard,
Nietzsche as well as Dante, Mallarmé as well as the
author of *Beowulf* or the *Odyssey*. If we look at the
actual operations of the poets they are surely charac-

terised by a highly selective indifference to large parts of this territory.

There is a way of reading this persuasive essay in which it commands an easy, almost unthinking assent. Our minds are prepared for it. Yes, one feels, here is Mr. Eliot saying in his own idiom just the sort of thing that Matthew Arnold said. And of course Arnold was right and was very good for us, and this is right and very good for us too. It is the perpetually needed antidote to Anglo-Saxon laziness and complacency and provincialism. But we have often reflected too that Arnold's programme was a programme for the man of culture rather than a programme for the poet. Of course poets have often been cultured men, and poetry has often been a learned art. But in essence the poet is not coincident with the cultured man; his plan of life is not the same. The cultured man is the transmitter of a tradition of civilisation, the poet is one of its makers. There will always be a need for a body of men with a profound awareness, the kind of awareness that is given only by learning, of our whole cultural tradition. But it is not likely that many of the poets will be of their number.

Behind this whole argument lies the question of whether tradition is something unconsciously inherited or something consciously acquired. And our answer to this will very considerably affect our feeling about the new Anglo-American poetry of the early twentieth

Imagist Poetry and the Tradition

century, with its self-consciousness, its acute sensitiveness to both precedent and novelty. Mr. Eliot distinguishes authentic tradition from the mere lazy acquiescence in the habits of our immediate predecessors; and the distinction is important. Perhaps it can be made clearer by analogies from other fields than literature. We have often seen movements, revivals undertaken in the name of tradition, that strike the official bearers of tradition as strange and offensive novelties. Consider the impact of Newman and the Oxford Movement on the old high-and-dry Anglican church; consider the puzzled scepticism with which Disraeli's Young England movement, its mixture of Carlyle and romantic medievalism, must have affected the old-fashioned county member; or consider in this country the Southern literary group, the Fugitives, traditionalist and regionalist in intention, yet with an avowed hostility to the embattled provincialism of the Old South. In each case the young movement claims to be representing a rediscovery of tradition in a purer and more authentic form, while its official representatives stand merely for a debased acquiescence. Something of the same sort seems to be implied in the talk about tradition that accompanied the rise of modern Imagist poetry. In all cases the claims abide our question. Who did really represent English religious tradition, Newman, or, say, Keble? Who did really represent the spirit of English Toryism, Disraeli or the hunting squire?

Imagist Poetry and the Tradition

Who is nearer to a central poetic tradition, Ezra Pound or Robert Frost? There is no standard answer to such questions. We can only examine each case on its merits.

Another view of tradition seems to make its appearance in Mr. Eliot's later writings. In *After Strange Gods* (1933) he distinguishes between "tradition," which is a matter of habit, local association, use and wont, and valuable for that very reason; and "orthodoxy," which is something that must be actively acquired and defended.[4] In *The Idea of a Christian Society* he speaks of the mass of humanity, mainly occupied by their direct relation to their daily duties and pleasures, whose capacity for *thinking* about the objects of their faith must be small. Of these he says "their Christianity may be almost wholly realised in behaviour; both in their customary and periodical religious observances, and in a traditional code of behaviour towards their neighbors."[5] I believe there is an analogical lesson for poetry here. In the sentences just quoted there is an implied contrast between the ordinary wayfaring Christian, whose faith is largely inherited, unconscious and inexplicit, and the theologian or intellectual defender of the faith who needs to be aware of its position in his civilisation as a whole, and of its historic origins. There is also, of course, though Mr. Eliot does not mention him, the saint; and it is possible that the saint may have more in common with the ordinary wayfaring Christian than with the theologian. His sanctity is more likely to reveal itself in behaviour, in his devotional life and in his relation to his neighbour than in speculation or learning. In poetry the analogue to the ordinary Christian is the common reader; the analogue to the theologian is the critic or the man of culture; the analogue to the saint is surely the poet. And both the poet and the saint may dispense with much of the historical consciousness, the acquired deliberate awareness of tradition, that to the theologian or the cultured critic is a necessity.

If we look at the ways poetic tradition has actually been transmitted I think we shall find that it has been in exactly the ways that Mr. Eliot says it can not be. Typically, the poet forms himself on one or two private admirations, as Keats did; or on a highly eccentric eclecticism, as Yeats did; or on a single preferred period, as the poets of Augustan England did. Surely the preponderant influence of one or two private admirations is a very noticeable feature of the work of Mr. Eliot himself. The conscientious and laborious taking of all culture as one's province is more characteristic of the scholar-poet, often quite a minor poet, such as Gray.

I believe that a poet's traditional quality, though it may be displayed and expounded by historical scholarship, actually realises itself in his relation to his readers, and in his relation to a certain community of human feeling—what Johnson called the "uniformity of sentiment" that underwrites poetic communication. The traditional poet, or any poet so far as he is traditional, addresses his readers in the confidence that he will be understood; that his rhetoric and his mode of address will be familiar to them from their previous reading of poetry; and he appeals to an order of feeling that he assumes to be common to himself and them, simply as human beings, or as members of a particular civilisation. When Wordsworth speaks in the preface to the *Lyrical Ballads,* not without bitterness, of the expectation that the poet "will gratify known habits of association" in his readers he is aware that he is not writing as a traditional poet, as far as his rhetoric is concerned; though of course he appeals to a very deep-rooted human tradition as far as his material is concerned. But Wordsworth, at this period of his life, is an extreme example of a poet trying to write as though no poetry has ever existed before. This is never possible; but it is necessary from time to time that the attempt should be made. There is always the temptation to equate "traditional" with "good," if we associate poetry with the ancient and enduring in our civilisation; or with "bad," if we associate poetry with revolution and novelty. But both are illegitimate; poetry is good or bad independently of whether it is traditional or not. All that we are concerned with now is to enquire how the traditional quality manifests itself, and to identify it where it occurs.

This is a traditional poem:

To Earthward

Love at the lips was touch
As sweet as I could bear;
And once that seemed too much;
I lived on air

That crossed me from sweet things,
The flow of—was it musk
From hidden grapevine springs
Down hill at dusk?

I had the swirl and ache
From sprays of honeysuckle
That when they're gathered shake
Dew on the knuckle.

I craved strong sweets, but those
Were strong when I was young;
The petal of the rose
It was that stung.

Now no joy but lacks salt
That is not dashed with pain
And weariness and fault;
I crave the stain

Of tears, the aftermark
Of almost too much love,
The sweet of bitter bark
And burning clove.

When stiff and sore and scarred
I take away my hand
From leaning on it hard
In grass and sand,

The hurt is not enough:
I long for weight and strength
To feel the earth as rough
To all my length.[6]

Imagist Poetry and the Tradition

It is traditional in spite of the fact that it has no obvious reference to previous poetry or current awareness of earlier models. It is traditional because it assumes easily and naturally that a reader whose habits have been formed on existing poetry in the same language will be able easily and naturally to respond to it. As Johnson said of some lines in Gray's "Elegy," "I have never seen the notions in any other place; yet he that reads them here, persuades himself that he has always felt them." With notable originality of turn and image, the poem appeals to a complex of feelings about the love of life in youth, and the approach of old age and death, that can be fairly called universal, that has at any rate often provided material for poetry before, in a great variety of ways. To touch on a detail—the slight, delicate, but quite marked and definite semantic shock given by the lines

> The petal of the rose
> It was that stung

seem to be an eminently traditional way of using language, of combining wit with feeling. I could say much the same thing of many of John Crowe Ransom's poems; but then they are very consciously traditional; he is well aware that he is re-writing "Gather ye rosebuds" or the epitaph on Salathiel Pavy. And my point is that a poem may be traditional simply by virtue of an established rhetoric and an established way

of feeling, without any apparent historical reference
or learning.

Now let us look at another kind of poem. Mr. C. S.
Lewis, in his inaugural lecture at Cambridge a few
years ago, posits the idea of a great rift, a break in
European culture, somewhere between the battle of
Waterloo and our own day. This is not a matter that
I wish to argue, it is not our present concern; but he
calls in evidence for his contention the nature of much
modern poetry. If we eliminate judgments of value
and concentrate on the historical fact, he writes, "I
do not see how any one can doubt that modern poetry
is not only a greater novelty than any other 'new
poetry' but new in a new way, almost in a new dimen-
sion. To say that all new poetry was once as difficult
as ours is false; to say that any was is an equivocation.
Some earlier poetry was difficult, but not in the same
way. Alexandrian poetry was difficult because it pre-
supposed a learned reader; as you became learned you
found the answers to the puzzles." After citing some
other examples he goes on: "I do not see in any of
these the slightest parallel to the state of affairs dis-
closed by a recent symposium on Mr. Eliot's 'A Cooking Egg.' Here we find seven adults (two of them
Cambridge men) whose lives have been specially
devoted to the study of poetry discussing a very short
poem which has been before the world for thirty-odd
years; and there is not the slightest agreement among

Imagist Poetry and the Tradition

them as to what, in any sense of the word, it means."[7]
The symposium in question was conducted in the
pages of an Oxford periodical, *Essays in Criticism*.[8] I
should like to add, in the interests of friendship, local
piety and truth, that the correct and sensible answer
seems to me to be given by one of the Cambridge men,
Dr. Tillyard; but what are we among so many? And
the point here is the diversity of opinion among
competent and qualified readers. The poem is very
familiar; it is the one that begins

> Pipit sate upright in her chair
> Some distance from where I was sitting;
> *Views of the Oxford College*
> Lay on the table, with the knitting.
>
> Daguerrotypes and silhouettes,
> Her grandfather and great-great aunts,
> Supported on the mantelpiece
> An *Invitation to the Dance*.

I will not go into the multiple confusions of the discussion. Some of them seem to me fatuous, others
merely ignorant. To confine ourselves to one—the
question of who Pipit is. It is variously suggested that
she is the speaker's old nurse, a little girl, a Blooms-
bury *demi-vierge,* his mistress, his fiancée, any *femme
de trente ans* whom he had known as a child. After all,
it makes a difference. I think Mr. Lewis has made his
point. This is a new thing, that a short poem of no
verbal intricacy should leave its contemporary readers
in a state of complete uncertainty as to what, in any

ordinary sense, it is "about." It is untraditional also in other ways. Not only has the tradition of an easy and immediate communication between writer and reader disappeared; the poem appeals to no permanent and established way of feeling. The rather uneasy superiority of the speaker to Pipit and her decor is not a relation of any depth or importance; and it is not part of any area of feeling with which European poetry has largely dealt. The semantic shock at the end, the contrast between "the eagles and the trumpets" and the weeping multitudes drooping in London tea-shops is mildly startling; but little more than verbally startling, for what is it, after all, but a version of the weak, modern-romantic-ironic contrast between ancient splendor and contemporary vulgarity? The poem is thickly decorated with historical references—Sir Philip Sidney, Coriolanus, Lucrezia Borgia, Madame Blavatsky, Piccarda de Donati; the verse form reminds one vaguely of Gautier, and the tone of Laforgue. But the wealth of cultural references will not persuade us that what we are in contact with here is the mind of Europe.

It is needless, probably, to say that I am not instituting a comparison between the poetical merits of Mr. Eliot and Mr. Frost; and if I were to undertake such an unprofitable task I should not use an early and rather trivial poem of Mr. Eliot's as an example. But though "A Cooking Egg" is not a fair example of achievement, it is a fair example of method, and of a kind of method that extends far beyond the work of Mr. Eliot. Similar illustrations could be drawn from the work of Pound, Wallace Stevens, not to mention younger writers such as Auden and Dylan Thomas. In all of them we find a host of examples where immediate communications between poet and reader fails on two planes; both on the plane of reference, all that is ordinarily called the "sense" of the poem; and on the plane of feeling, the emotional attitude towards the situation presented. Whatever tradition Imagist poetry may have recalled us to, the most important tradition of all, that of a natural community of understanding between poet and reader, has been lost.

In the face of these obscure breakdowns of communication criticism has almost capitulated. Or rather, it has turned with relief to other tasks than judgment. The best modern criticism has made surprisingly little attempt to judge the most challenging contemporary literature, to estimate its value, or what can amount to the same thing, to place it properly in relation to the literature of the past. We are always hearing about this being done, and that it should be done—the existing monuments form an ideal order to which the new work will be seen to attach itself, to form a changed yet continuous pattern. But in fact most of the criticism has concentrated on the novelty rather than the continuity, in panegyric, extenuation, exegesis—everything in fact from log-rolling to what is called explication.

The value judgments on the whole have not been made. Modern literature—and modern literature in this context still tends to mean what began in 1914—has become and remained a sort of enclave in the critical tradition, with its own laws and its own ways of interpreting them. Where these writings stand in the general comity of letters has hardly been asked, with any seriousness or pertinacity, still less answered.

There are several reasons for this, some of them entirely generous ones. A novel kind of imaginative writing is commonly exposed to ignorance, abuse and vociferous inertia. When this is going on it is more important to get the new work fairly read than to decide on its ultimate position in a hierarchy. It mattered more in the twenties to get *The Waste Land* read with some degree of sympathy and open-mindedness than to decide on its status in relation to *In Memoriam* or Pope's *Moral Essays*. At such times the most immediately necessary criticism is a kind of propaganda or block-busting for new creative work. If more is attempted it is on a very narrow front. The work is explained on its own terms, and justified by its own standards; but not much attempt is made to apply standards derived from our literary experience as a whole. A symptom of this is the inability to stand outside our own phase of civilisation. The words plight and dilemma do especially heavy duty. *The Waste Land* (or *Finnegans Wake* or *Hugh Selwyn Mauber-*

ley or whatever it may be) presents the plight of our
time, in the methods of our time. If it seems to be
confused, well, so are we. There is an interesting
example of this method in the closing pages of that
invaluable piece of commentary, the *Skeleton Key to
Finnegans Wake:*

> In some quarters it is the fashion to dismiss Joyce
> with various charges, all pivoting on the word 'decad-
> ent.' He is a solipsist talking to himself in a nutshell
> kingdom of his own. He is a sick spirit addicted to
> pathologic gnawings of no possible interest to those
> of us with splendid, robust minds. . . . He is a man
> who has lost his faith and whose world is a living
> doomsday, a bleak pit of pessimism.
> If Joyce is sick, his disease is the neurosis of our
> age. Lifting our eye from his page we find in every
> aspect of society the perversion, the decay, and the
> disintegration of religion, love and morality that he has
> described in Finnegan's Wake. The hypocrisy of politi-
> cal promises, the prurient preoccupation with sex, the
> fascination of lurid headlines gossip and its effect on a
> literate but basically ignorant bourgeoisie—all these
> are mirrored to the life by this liveliest of observers.
> . . . If Joyce's viewpoint is pathologic, then any rosier
> lens is sentimental.[9]

The words decadent and sick have not much meaning here without further elucidation; but that is not
the point. The point is that the critical argument is a
simple *tu quoque.* "Joyce a decadent? Yah, you're
another." Joyce is justified, not by showing that he has
created out of his material a rational or aesthetically
satisfying order, but by the claim that he reproduces

faithfully the disorder inherent in his material. By this standard the artist becomes a tape-recorder to the Zeitgeist; his success is in the completeness and finality of his reproduction.

Of course the main object of the *Skeleton Key* is to elucidate, and the passage I have quoted is only incidental to its purpose. And much of the best criticism of modern literature has been of this kind—the providing of readers' guides to difficult works. The guides were needed, and some of them are serious and assiduous to the last degree. The best are probably those that keep most closely to the primary task of smoothing out difficulties of communication, and stick to the informative and demonstrable—do in fact what a good edition of an ancient classic would do. The danger in commenting on works with such density of reference as much modern poetry is that the immediate impact of the poetry is dulled by the circumambient mass of erudition. The reader is like the hi-fi enthusiast—he is too busy fiddling with the machinery to get the best out of the music.

One of the most striking recent literary developments is the independent emergence of criticism, I will not say as an autonomous art, but as something between a profession and big business. So far as it is a profession, criticism has developed its own standards of expertise and technique; and it has become easy to pass from the useful task of writing guide-books to the elaboration of commentaries, generally ingenious and sometimes of dazzling virtuosity, which still do little or nothing to deepen appreciation of the poetry; and being without standards except those derived internally from the work itself, do little to extend the area of critical order. So far as it is big business, criticism is highly competitive; every interpretation evokes a rival one; and the topic of discussion becomes A's qualification of B's attack on C's elucidation of whatever the original object may have been. Meanwhile the original object has got tacitly taken for granted; the original questions about its value and meaning have slipped out of sight.

There is another reason why explanation of obscure works has been preferred to judgment; and it is a genial one. A consequence of the prevailing Imagist technique and of Joyce's exploitation of multiple verbal ambiguities is that much of modern literature gives great local delight even when its general purport remains obscure. And judgment must be of a work as a whole—ultimately of its whole bearing and direction. Yet it often seems churlish or ungrateful to disturb or question much of the whole foundations of a work that has given intense pleasure in detail. No one sensitive to language (and most modern critics are extremely sensitive to language) can fail to be dazzled, delighted, and sometimes moved by the verbal felicities of *Finnegans Wake* or the fragmentary fine passages in the

Cantos, whether or not he has any idea of how they are related to their context, or what the context is. Not only that: the Imagist method, and Joyce's rather different method of accumulating cartloads of particulars are both profoundly sensual; they make a direct assault on the nerves and the perceptions. They hit the reader between wind and water with a piercing sensational bombardment, in a way that literature depending more on logical or narrative connection can never do. The delight given is more akin to physical pleasure than to "thoughts more elevate of providence, foreknowledge, will and fate." I am not referring at all to subject-matter, merely to the consequences of a poetic method. Prolonged attention to the works of this school becomes in the end more like an addiction or a fetishism than an ordinary literary experience, simply because of this concentrated battery of small sensuous shocks. The quality of addiction or fetishism reveals itself in the inability to consider seriously any other source of literary pleasure; the constant assertions, for example, that in the nineteenth century language was in decay; "Tennyson and Browning ruminated," "the bankrupt's lavishness with which Morris and Swinburne dispense their tinfoil counters." The less immediate and sensational literary experiences, if they are present at all, are decidedly in the background. These shocks of sensuous recognition, more thickly sown, because of the Imagist method, in the literature of our century than in any other, are the sharpest pleasures that poetry has to give; and one who has felt them does not wish to dull or depreciate their setting (though he frequently conceals the nature of his appreciation under a forbiddingly puritan demeanour). And the critic confines himself to providing a minimum framework in which they can be enjoyed without nagging objections from the discursive intellect; or in a justifiable eagerness to make the most of the parts which have delighted him, plays down the importance of total communicated meaning—the meaning that can only be communicated through structure.

The most fantastic example of this procedure is provided (as one might expect) by Hugh Kenner. He defends Pound's ideographic method by the following parallel: "Six months after reading *King Lear* one's memory, one's sense of its vital reality, consists perhaps in recalling that a storm is followed by a pathetic death. We don't remember the plot as set forth in handbooks. . . . Memory automatically strips any intense experience down to its poetic essentials, a few vivid juxtapositions."[10] It is hard to suppose that Mr. Kenner really believes that the connection between the scenes of a Shakespearean tragedy is of the same kind as the connection between Pound's "ideograms"; hard to believe that a critic who constantly postures as an Aristotelian and has presumably read the *Poetics* can bring himself to say it. But he does say it; and even a very different writer, perhaps the most serious and responsible critic of modern poetry that we have, R. P. Blackmur, after having almost squarely faced the consequences of the rag-bag quality of the *Cantos,* shys off at the end and reduces the gravity of his conclusions by a sneer at the common reader. He concludes his essay "Masks of Ezra Pound" with these words: " 'A catalogue, his jewels of conversation.' The *Cantos* are an anthology of such jewels and read as most people read anthologies, as indeed all but a few read any sort of poetry, for the felicity of line and phrase, for strangeness, or for an echoed aptness of sentiment, the reader can afford to forget the promise and ambition of which the poem cheated him. He will have been equally cheated in all but the smallest part of his reading."[11] But this is quite untrue. The cases are not parallel. The reader of an anthology reads whole poems. He may flit uncritically and unhistorically among them; but each exists in its own right; each communicates to him as a whole. This is not the experience of a reader of the *Cantos*. There are magnificent lines and passages indeed; but they are rarely whole poems; they are almost all fragmentary, or blurred at the edges, or contaminated, either with rubbish or with alien matter. I do not see that the anthology sipper is cheated at all as he goes from a Shakespeare sonnet to the "Coy Mistress" to "Mariana" in the *Oxford Book of English Verse;* but if he is cheated it is in a wholly different way from the exasperated reader of the *Cantos* finding what satisfaction he can in splendid or beautiful fragments, neither complete in themselves nor having any intelligible connection with a larger whole. Only the wilful blindness of addiction could lead this admirable critic to append a false conclusion to the judgment he has made.

A similar trope is employed by Mr. Kenner again. The *Cantos* have been found disconnected, incoherent and obscure. Very well, then: "Probably very few graduate students enjoy a confident, other than habitual, assurance of the presence of connection between the two stanzas of the familiar 'Lucy' poem," "A slumber did my spirit seal."[12] It is symptomatic of Mr. Kenner's culture that the only persons he can think of as likely readers of Wordsworth are graduate students, and that the handiest way he can find to get out of a tight spot is to belabor his pupils. But even if his suggestion were true, and even if the condition of Mr. Kenner's graduate students were of any importance in the general context of European letters, how would all this make the *Cantos* any better? This technique of non-explanation is continued in his third appendix, "The Cantos; Further Notes"; notes which merely paraphrase confusion— a set of muddled jottings which are supposed to represent the "themes" of the poem, and do nothing whatever to show that the themes combine into an intelligible order.

Imagist Poetry and the Tradition

Time after time we find that the major critical questions that modern literature ought to arouse are left virtually unattempted. The honourable exception is in the work of Mr. Yvor Winters, who has subjected Imagist poetic theory, and its poetic practice, and the relation between the two, to a searching and stern examination. I could not hope to emulate the rigour with which he has performed his task; it is only to be regretted that the devastating accuracy of his analysis has been partly obscured by some extremely eccentric judgments of individual poets, and what seems to me an untenable view of the moral relations of poetry. But in the ability to stand back and see twentieth-century poetry in a historical perspective, Mr. Winters stands alone. Others, with all their sensibility, industry and acumen have been docile followers of a rather elderly Zeitgeist. We are left with a crowd of claqueurs, bemused epigoni, Hudson Reviewers, wedding guests, each helplessly fascinated by his own Ancient Mariner; or morose bystanders who retain detachment at the price of insensibility. It is a paradox that today, when criticism is more active, more strenuous and better equipped than it has ever been, it has never managed to see the most typical work of its own time in the light of a mature literary experience.

Some reasons for this state of affairs have been suggested—reasons connected with the special kind of enjoyment that modern poetry gives. But there is I think another one; the real roots of the novelty in modern literary practice have been very little examined. We shall find the roots of English Imagist poetry in the French Symbolist area, the area that is bounded by Mallarmé and Rimbaud. And this is well enough known. Mr. Eliot has acknowledged his discipleship to Laforgue and Corbière; both Eliot and Pound in the early days made great play with Rémy de Gourmont; and there is a valuable study by René Taupin of Imagist-Symbolist relations.[13] But these known linkages seem to have made little impression on the general critical consciousness. Mr. Eliot's encomium on the Metaphysical Poets obscured the fact that his poetical methods have very little in common with theirs; and the extreme Anglican decorum of much of his critical writing has not inclined us to look towards Paris of the eighties for the origins of the new poetry. And Pound's odd and dazzling collection of antiquities—his exhortations to read Provençal, to read Guido Cavalcanti, to read Golding's translations of Ovid, to read Confucius—have brought about more bewilderment than illumination. Where there is a recognition of the powerful Symbolist spell it is apt to fall into the opposite excess of assuming that the Mallarmé-Rimbaud complex is the type of normal poetic situation. A recent study which I have encountered assumes quite openly that Mallarmé's *Coup de Dés* and *Finnegans Wake* are the two great monuments of modern Western culture. For a less extreme example we could turn to Miss Elizabeth Sewell who proposes to enquire into the structure of poetry in general (*The Structure of Poetry* is the title of her book) precisely by examining the work of Mallarmé and Rimbaud. She finds that Mallarmé pushes poetry as far as it can go towards the abstract and ordered structure of mathematics, Rimbaud towards the disordered concreteness of dream. And these, she suggests, are the two poles between which poetry exists, Number and Nightmare. Number and Nightmare—a splendid fragment of oracular incantation; but it seems odd to use these two extravagant indices to point out the normal structure of poetry. It is as if to say, to one who would inform himself on the nature of man: "Some people are mathematical logicians, others are delirious. You had better examine these two cases, for normal human experience lies between them."

The disordered concreteness of dream which Miss Sewell calls Nightmare is illustrated by her mainly from Rimbaud's *Bateau Ivre* and *Illuminations;* we could illustrate it too from *The Waste Land,* the *Cantos,* from large parts of *Ulysses* and from *Finnegans Wake.* It is essentially the Imagist method, some of whose consequences we have discussed. To turn now for a brief glance at the opposite extreme, Number, Mallarmé's method, the effort to turn poetry into a self-contained structure divorced as far as possible from concrete referential content. I am acutely aware that anything one says about Mallarmé may be wrong. Attempts to wrestle with Mallarmé's poetry, and some reading of what much better qualified critics, both French and English, have said about it, reveal such a diversity of possible judgments that one cannot feel very much confidence in saying anything. It is quite certain, however, that aspiration towards an impossible "purity," a liberation of poetry from all reference to the actual world, is a constant movement in Mallarmé. His critical writing everywhere reveals this. The question that remains is how can poetry move in this direction; how did Mallarmé think it could be approached? I say approached, for obviously this purity cannot be achieved. Words have meanings, references to things that are not words, and these references are inescapable. Pure poetry is always a mirage. Miss Sewell's answer is a simple one, and it is manifestly wrong. She supposes that Mallarmé attempts to make his poetry a pure structure of sounds, or since poetry is now generally read from the printed page, of sounds and appearances—what she calls the sound-look aspect of words. She sees in Mallarmé's poetry an intricate pattern of sounds and syllables, partly constituted by the exacting rhyme-schemes of his sonnets, partly by a system of internal rhyme, assonance and alliteration. Certainly this system is there and can be examined. Equally certainly it is grossly inadequate as an explanation of how the poems are constituted. This is revealed by the miserable poverty of the analyses that her method enables her to give. All she can find to say of a sonnet like "Le vierge, le vivace et le bel aujourd'hui" is:

> The essential of this poem is the i pattern. The rhymes make this clear at once, the octet rhyming on ui and ivre, the sestet on ie and igne. No line is without its i sound. . . . Added to it is the v pattern. This starts by being intimately associated with the i. . . .[14]

And so on. This is not nonsense; it is a part of the structure of the poem: but if, as she suggests, it *is* the structure of the poem, such poetry could not have the slightest interest for any rational being.

And of course this is not Mallarmé's procedure. His intelligence is far too subtle ever to have supposed that such an infantile simplification could have been more than an auxiliary to his purpose. If I may attempt a suggestion where so many better informed writers have made suggestions already, it is that Mallarmé endeavours to make poetry a paradigm for an experience, without the actual content. He tries to give, with the minutest delicacy, the structure of an experience without the actual experience; a structure that might be filled out, if we insist on filling it out, with many actual experiences. But the poem does not commit itself to any of them, or concern itself with them except in a minimal unavoidable way. Mallarmé's work has been described as a kind of poetical algebra. I have often wondered whether people who use this phrase know what they mean by it. But it will be clear, I imagine, what I might mean by it. Algebra performs structural operations without concerning itself with the actual value of the symbols it employs: Mallarmé's poetry tries to do something of this kind. Or we can use the analogy (it has more than once been consecrated to poetic purposes) of a jar, whose shape is beautiful, satisfactory, complete—and can be filled indifferently with ashes, brandy, weak tea, water or nothing at all.

Mallarmé's sonnet "M'introduire dans ton histoire" has given rise to a number of explanations, and its last line "Du seul vespéral de mes chars" became at one time a proverbial phrase for the sonorous unintelligible gibberish of which his poetry was supposed by its enemies to be made up. The poem has been variously seen as an ingeniously veiled obscenity, as a less indecorous piece, but still on an erotic theme; as the account of an imaginary triumph after a real amorous failure; of a real triumph after coldness and disappointment. The scene from which it takes its departure has been variously figured as the intimate meeting-place of two lovers, a carriage going for a drive in the evening, and a firework display. This will be enough to illustrate the dubieties that are possible in reading the poem, and the impossibility of assigning to it a definite referential content. What then remains? A structure; partly indeed a structure of sounds and syllables such as that suggested by Miss Sewell; but also a structure of meaning—timidity, the sense of sanctities violated, the chill of repulsion and failure, followed by a grandiose triumph. How does Mallarmé contrive to keep his poem in this state of abstraction, without unduly arousing —and certainly without satisfying—the reader's ordinary desire for a concrete content? Partly (though more in some other sonnets than in this one) by an elaborate deformation of syntax which absolutely prevents the reading of the poem as anything approaching narrative or description; partly by using metaphor and image in such a way that the tenor of the metaphor (what it might convey in a prose paraphrase) is left uncertain or undiscoverable. One example must suffice, a metaphorical phrase to which it is almost impossible to assign a literal meaning because it couples together incomparable classes of objects. "Tonnerre et rubis aux moyeux"; thunder and rubies at the axle-trees. We cannot locate *thunder* and *rubies* together in any imagined physical space. When Mr. Eliot adapts this phrase—

> Garlic and sapphires in the mud
> Clot the bedded axle-tree

—he is less bold. Garlic and sapphires are both material objects, they can be found in the same mud in which a wheel is supposed to be buried. True, the metaphor still has to be interpreted, but we are not dazzled at the start by a coruscating obliquity on its surface. Thunder and rubies together are a sort of no-road sign, forbidding access to a referential meaning. And this no doubt is only one of many devices by which Mallarmé, while preserving a structural relation between different parts of the poem, prevents us from giving it a defined content.

Mallarmé remains the extreme example of this kind of poetic effect; but it has though less consistently become a familiar feature of modern poetry in English. Even "A Cooking Egg" affords a slight illustration—we know Pipit's position in the poem, her relative status, even if we do not know who or what she is. We could find the same sort of thing in parts of Auden's work; but for clearer and more abundant examples we should look in the poetry of Wallace Stevens. The parallel between him and Mallarmé has often been remarked. Of course the deliberate exploitation of such effects is a very specialised, very recent, and very untypical development in poetry. They are far remote from the main poetic stream. Epic and dramatic poetry could not proceed in this way; and most lyric does not. Nightmare and number may, as Elizabeth Sewell suggests, be the two poles of poetic experience, but the exploration of each of them simply draws us away from the great temperate area in between where nearly all poetry has its being. And this brings us back, after a long excursion, to our original subject, poetry and tradition. In spite of much talk of tradition, the characteristic, idiosyncratic features of twentieth-century poetry have taken it away (in a phrase which I quote from Mr. M. H. Abrams) from "the central tradition of poetics, which looked upon poetry not as a verbal structure nor (in C. Day Lewis's phrase) as an image composed of images, but as a verbal representation, artistically ordered, of thinking, feeling and acting human beings."[15]

Crystal-gazing as a critical method had better be reduced to a minimum; but it is hard to believe that poetry in the future can make any further progress in the Imagist-Symbolist direction. If it were to remain in that mode it would either lead a fading invalidish life and then die altogether, or become an esoteric plaything. Either could happen. Then, if I were one of the morose depreciators of modern poetry that I fear I have often made myself sound like, I should proceed to say that this whole experiment has been a dead end, and that poetry must retrace its steps. But this is not what I want to say. If we are to use metaphors, mine would not be a *cul-de-sac* but a detour, a diversion from the main road. Traffic along the main road has been proceeding all the time, and we do not sufficiently remember this. In talking of modern poetry we ought to recall more often than we do that Hardy was writing till 1926, and that among the poets of our century are Robert Frost, Robert Graves, John

Crowe Ransom, Edwin Muir and John Betjeman. But the detour has been considerable, and most of the heavy traffic has chosen to travel on it. It is probably time it rejoined the main highway. But, to abandon the metaphor, which is becoming inconvenient, it is no use imagining that things will ever be the same again. This is like the social illusion of going back to pre-war days, with which we used to delude ourselves for a short time after 1918, and have abandoned forever, ever since. All we can say is that some of the most brilliant poetic innovations of the most original poetic talents of our day are probably inimitable and unrepeatable. They cannot be developed any farther, and they have been of a kind from which it is very difficult to learn. Yet they cannot be forgotten or ignored. This I believe is the difficult situation that poetry finds itself in today.

III.

The Nature of a Revolution

A few years ago, when the *Rock-Drill* section of Pound's *Cantos* appeared, a reviewer justly remarked that the most part of it is simply not poetry in English. After some further commentary on this cento of Greek, Latin, French and Italian tags, Chinese ideograms and Egyptian hieroglyphs, all pressed into an English setting, he concluded by saying "This is the poetry of the future." A Johnsonian phrase seems called for: surely while his breath was forming this proposition into words his understanding must have suspected it to be ridiculous. Perhaps it was intended only as a pious hyperbole. Prophecy is not a useful subject for debate; we can only usefully inquire by what motive it was prompted. Evidently there is some loss of faith in poetry written in English (or presumably in any one language), some sort of belief that the future of poetry is bound up with a composite polyglot discourse. What Wyndham Lewis called the Demon of Progress in the arts is still at work. Here as often he operates by making lunatic extrapolations from events that have actually occurred. There is not the slightest evidence that the integrity of individual linguistic traditions is weakening, or that poetry could live and transmit itself through a jumble of half-comprehended multilingual fragments. But this is an inference, if it is anything so respectable, from a real historical development—from the fact that the English literary community has undergone a great expansion in this century.

I want to return to this topic in a moment, but first I would dwell briefly on a few social-economic platitudes and their implications for literature. Literature is among other things a commodity; and if one had deciphered the Coca-Cola signs in Arabic script along the shores of the Suez Canal, read advertisments for Nestlé's milk in Malay newspapers, bought Gillette razor-blades in Hanoi, Lucky Strikes in Innsbruck, or Courvoisier brandy in Chicago, one cannot doubt that commodities today have an international range. Once we get above the level of the merest domestic subsistence, we live in a culture that is no longer regional, no longer national, but composite and eclectic, and therefore becoming steadily more uniform. This cosmopolitan civilisation based on science, technology and social democracy, can be regarded with complacency or with misgiving. We can point to the enrichment and variety of experience that it makes possible in any one particular spot; we can point too to the fact that one spot begins to look very much like another. Of course we want to have our cake and eat it. The great international capital where everything can be had and anything may happen is one of the achievements of our civilisation; but we cannot wish it to become the universal model. We want our own region and the regions that we visit to retain their individual qualities. Provincialism is deeply rooted in our nature. We have all known those peasants of London, Paris or New York, who can hardly conceive of life outside the bounds of their brick and concrete *pays*. It would be a melancholy state if peace were only to be secured by making everywhere exactly like everywhere else. But of course uniformity does not imply agreement. Two dogs of the same breed are just as likely to fight over a bone as two different ones; and to be oneself makes it no more likely that one will want to quarrel with one's neighbour.

The international exchanges, cultural missions and conferences in which our world abounds have probably done nothing to bring about a unity of culture; and if they did they would do nothing to bring about international agreement. There is really no political argument for internationalising culture and the arts. Some of the arts are by their nature more capable of international diffusion—music and painting, most happily. We have an international style of architecture at present —much less happily, for a variety of reasons. But literature, tied to language as it is, is absolutely prevented from developing in the same way; and technology and communications hardly affect the situation.

The Nature of a Revolution

This huge mongrelised commercial civilisation, living on the same products, made in the same factories, sold out of similar shops, is powerless before the fact of language. By the mercy of heaven, French literature remains French, Italian literature remains Italian, and English literature remains English. And contacts between them seem to be of the same nature as they have always been—fertilising, refreshing, but no more massive and tending no more to standardisation than they were in the sixteenth century or the eighteenth. This is the great bulwark against the dreary entropy of taste that is rapidly afflicting cookery, building and interior decoration.

It is the language barrier, the blessed and almost total failure of such projects as Esperanto and Basic English, that guarantee continued diversity. Within a single linguistic area it is harder to see what is actually going on, and far harder to know what state of affairs is to be desired. In this respect the English linguistic area is unique. More than any other, English is a world language. A greater number of people speak Chinese; but they are nearly all in China, and belong to a common culture. Users of English are scattered all over the globe, and belong to enormously differing social and cultural systems. This has been the case for long enough. The English linguistic community has been growing steadily for over two hundred years. And yet I spoke of the English *literary* community undergoing a great and rapid change in this century; and I think this is true. Until recently many parts of the English-speaking world were hardly parts of a literary community at all, whether as producers or consumers. They are now active in both directions. And America, which was always a literary community from the time of the first settlers, has had an enormous expansion of its literary public and its literary consciousness in the last fifty years. The result of these developments is that English writing is a commodity of international diffusion as writing in no other language can be. And this has had a profound though not easily defineable effect on the literature of our century.

The greatest realignment of forces has been in Anglo-American literary relations. They have become completely transformed in the last fifty years; and this has had both a broad general effect on the sense of values, and a quite specific effect on the modern literary revolution that we have been discussing. If we are to discover the nature of our recent poetic upheaval we must pay some attention to these circumstances. I am persuaded that there is a massive cultural phenomenon here that has not yet been properly examined—still not properly examined, in spite of the establishment of American literature as an academic discipline, and the conscientious exhortations in the London *Times Literary Supplement* to recognize its existence. It is not a question of recognising its exist-

The Nature of a Revolution

ence, but of realising its effect on the whole English-speaking literary community. Up to some time in the middle of the nineteenth century American literature was not so much subordinated to English as a part of it. It drew its standards and its style from English sources, and it had a quite straightforward appeal to an English audience. On late-Victorian English book-shelves Emerson stood beside Carlyle, and Longfellow beside Tennyson. I suppose no one can date exactly the beginning of a separate American literary personality. The programme is outlined in Emerson's "American Scholar" lecture of 1837, and his other lecture "The Poet" of seven years later; and the programme preceded the performance. However much of the American spirit and material may have appeared in earlier writing, what a European would recognize as a distinct American style in poetry appears only with Whitman, and in prose only with Mark Twain. But the distinct American style does make its appearance, and from that time on the question of the relationship between American and English literature has been active. A robust British Victorian view of the matter is expressed by Matthew Arnold.

> I see advertised *The Primer of American Literature.* Imagine the face of Philip or Alexander at hearing of a primer of Macedonian Literature! . . . We are all contributors to one great literature—English Literature.[1]

This is not quite the proprietorial pronouncement

that it sounds; Arnold is merely asserting the primacy of language in the cultural tradition, and its power to override local differences. And this is not self-evidently absurd. But both Emerson and Whitman saw the matter otherwise. And surely by now there is no longer anything to argue about—as a mere question of fact. There is an American literature, distinct in its material, its characteristic interest and to a large extent in its style from English literature. At present its power in the world is a good deal greater.

But once we let go of the mere fact and begin to consider its implications there is a great deal that still needs enquiry and understanding. In all the discussion of American literature and its status it has never I think been remarked, on either side of the Atlantic, that we have here a cultural situation unique in the history of the world. We have two civilisations, widely different in social habits, political assumptions, and relation to the international community, producing two different literatures, but in the same language, and having behind them a common literary heritage. I do not believe that there is any stage in the history of our civilisation when a situation quite like this has prevailed. There is no real parallel in the Hellenistic or Imperial Roman world. We have seen provincial and colonial styles appearing in a metropolitan literature. But this is something quite different. American writers are not in the position of Apuleius or Seneca or St.

Augustine. They are writing in English, with a background of English literature—but out of an established, unified and quite un-English civilisation. The only similar relation is that between the Spanish literature of Spain and that of the Spanish speaking countries in the New World. This is less striking, for the civilisation of Latin America is not a unified one like that of the United States; and the relation is in any case only another instance of the same distinctively new state of affairs.

So far as Emerson and Whitman were only proclaiming their right to a distinctively American subject-matter they were not saying anything particularly controversial. A new country offers new material. And shorn of the patriotic rhetoric, some of their claims amount to no more than this. When Emerson says that the American writer should see in "the barbarism and materialism" of his own day "another carnival of the same gods whose picture he so much admires in Homer" he is saying what may be doubted, but he means little more than that America has the right to make an epic of its own matter if it can. "America is a poem in our eyes; its ample geography dazzles the imagination, and it will not wait long for meters."[2] But when the meters, if not precisely Homeric ones, actually arrive with Whitman, hardly more than ten years later, they make a larger claim for themselves. Whitman writes in the preface to *Leaves of Grass,*

The Nature of a Revolution

"The Americans of all nations at any time upon the earth have probably the fullest poetical nature. The United States themselves are essentially the greatest poem."[3] There is implicit in these words not only the announcement of a new subject-matter, but a new scale of literary values. It is repeated in *Democratic Vistas:*[4] "America demands a poetry that is bold, modern and all-surrounding and cosmical, as she is herself. . . . Erect, inflated and fully self-esteeming be the chant; and then America will listen with pleased ears." And then we turn back and realise that the new scale of values had already been announced by Emerson himself. Acknowledging that the ideal poet has not yet appeared in America, Emerson also fails to find him in five centuries of English poetry. "These are wits rather than poets, though there have been poets among them. But when we adhere to the ideal of the poet, we have our difficulties even with Milton and Homer. Milton is too literary, and Homer too literal and historical."[5] There is to be an improved scale of values for America, then, by which Milton and Homer will be insufficient.

And that is the real problem raised by the emergence of a second literature in the English language. Linguistically it cannot help inheriting five centuries of English literary tradition—a tradition always vitally connected with that of Europe as a whole. And yet so far as it is a new literature springing from a new world it is socially and experientially unrelated to much of the English tradition. I think there can be no doubt that a distinctly American set of literary values has emerged in recent years; and that its co-presence with European ones is still capable of causing bewilderment. An Englishman in America cannot help being aware that a number of shrines in the literary pantheon command very different degrees of devotion in the two countries. If the status of Henry James is internationally agreed, that of Hawthorne, Melville and Thoreau is not. They do not assume much importance in the English literary imagination; and Henry Adams none at all. American literature is a much more national affair than English has ever been or felt itself to be. Writers are esteemed for their American quality, for their share in establishing a peculiarily American consciousness, and a good deal of what goes on in the study of American literature seems to the outsider to belong to social rather than to literary history. On the other hand the Englishman becomes intermittently conscious that there are areas of the English literature of the past that look quite different to Americans, who stand outside the English social hierarchy, have no nostalgia for fogs and gaslight, and are not accustomed to babble of green fields.

The difficulties that this state of affairs may lead to can be illustrated from a recent critical study by Mr. Richard Chase. His important book *The American*

Novel and its Tradition sets out to define a specially American kind of novel. Mr. Chase, following Hawthorne, describes it as the "romance-novel," and to this category he finds that the greatest American fiction belongs. It diverges from the English tradition and cannot be accounted for by English literary standards; it diverges even from the traditions of classical tragedy and Christianity, which Mr. Chase sees to lie behind the work of the English novelists. His aim then is to isolate a distinct literary kind, with its own quality. Yet his definition is couched in terms that suggest mainly deficiency. The romance-novel as he describes it sounds like something that does not quite manage to become a novel of the ordinary sort. The word romance, he says, in this context, "must signify, besides the more obvious qualities of the picturesque and the heroic, an assumed freedom from the ordinary novelistic requirements of verisimilitude, development and continuity; a tendency towards melodrama and idyll . . . a willingness to abandon moral questions, or to ignore the spectacle of man in society, or to consider these things only indirectly and abstractly." And again, "Like other romance-novels, *Moby Dick* is thus somewhat disqualified for engaging the moral imagination in the sort of close involvement with real life which makes the context for moral ideas in such novels as those of Balzac, George Eliot or James himself."[6] Now, melodrama is an inferior form, idyll a slight one; a

willingness to abandon moral questions and a failure
to engage the moral imagination with real life sound
like serious disqualifications; and the compensatory
merits of the romance-novel sound more like special
pleading than a real balancing factor.

Yet as the book goes on the reader is mildly sur-
prised to find that these apparent deficiencies have
only to be seen as part of a distinctively American
tradition to be immediately transformed into virtues.
It is not necessary to say that something bad does not
become good by becoming American; or that this is
not what Mr. Chase intends to convey. If the romance-
novel is an independent form, as I have no doubt it is
(there are English and French examples of it as well
as American ones—*Wuthering Heights* and *Le Grand
Meaulnes* occur immediately to mind), it has its own
standards and its own kind of integrity. One does not
define *The Tempest* by its unlikeness to *Antigone*.
This is just one example of the sort of difficulties that
the dubious relation between English and American
literary values can lead us into.

My own conviction is that the difference in standards should be simply accepted. This sounds like a
pusillanimous agreement to differ; and since I do
not mean that, I should say welcomed, rather than
accepted. There should always be debate, as there
always has been in the European literary tradition; but
real debate, which recognises that the two parties start

from different points. This is only to recognise the obvious. Surely by now it is inevitable that out of the vast number of literary possibilities England should continue to interest itself in some that mean little to America, and that America should have selected or created others which are outside the English literary sphere.

Yet there was a period, and a very recent one, when it seemed that a common Anglo-American literary community with a common set of values was likely to develop. It was a period when the ascendant values were formalist ones—those which most easily transcend local and national difference. It is the period with which we are particularly concerned, that of our recent poetical revolution. There was a decade or so when all the newest and most promising poetry being written in English was written by Americans; but they had to come to England to do it. It is remarkable, one might note in parenthesis, that Robert Frost had to find an English publisher before his peculiarly American genius could make itself known. But of course I am thinking of the revolutionary work of Pound and Eliot. Pound in his early days preserved a passionate interest in the destinies of American poetry. He kept up continuous contacts with Harriet Monroe and her Chicago periodical *Poetry;* and with William Carlos Williams. He was always on the look-out for new American talent. Yet he lived in London, was much inclined for some years to talk of London as the cultural capital, and most of his early work appeared in English periodicals and editions. Mr. Eliot's destiny from 1915 onwards was far more exclusively linked to the English scene. No doubt the example of Henry James counted for much. He was revered by both Pound and Eliot, and he is the one great example of a writer whose status is equally assured on both sides of the Atlantic and who drew equal nourishment from the old and the new. But the brilliant and shimmering edifice he constructed is a sort of rainbow bridge, connecting the two worlds, kept up by miracle, and affording no foundation for later building. The post-Jacobean period of Anglo-American literary alliance seems to be an even less substantial structure.

The two American poets who were radically changing the direction of poetry in English were, it is true, expatriates, but they were expatriate Americans; and that means that their relation to the European poetic tradition was radically different from that of any English poet of their own time, or of any other time. The situation I am trying to describe is initially a matter of simple geography, but the cultural effects are more complicated. When an American goes abroad he is apt to say he is going to Europe. An Englishman says he is going to Paris or Austria or Florence. He can't go to Europe since he is in it already. From the Western side of the Atlantic Europe is apt to appear as a large geographical and cultural block, set over against America. From England, peripheral though its European position may be, Europe can never appear in this light. Indeed the Englishman has a rather feeble sense of Europe; he is inclined to think merely of particular places, whose acquaintance he makes gradually and sporadically. This is the crude origin of the difference I wish to point to, but it has manifold consequences in the literary field. Some of them are massive and obvious—the greater openness of America to a variety of European influences, for instance; some of them are subtle, extending to delicate details of poetic technique and expression.

There is a whole chapter of cultural history here, and this is not the place even to outline it. Let me instead look for a generalisation and a few pertinent examples. If we shift our ground from physical to mental travel we find an exact analogy. When the mental traveller from England makes his explorations into other European cultures he remains an Englishman who has connected his own literature and civilisation with some of its ancestors and collaterals. The American who moves away from his native grass-roots tends to become at one bound a cosmopolitan. His education encourages him to be so. Consider the number of college courses called Masterpieces, or Great Books, or World Literature, or something of that kind—in which the undergraduate is given in a single year a guided tour around the great monuments of European culture from the *Iliad* to *Finnegans Wake.* When Pound first came to Europe he was a graduate student in Romance languages. It is not easy for an Englishman to be a graduate student in Romance languages, for the educational system does not encourage the blunderbuss study of a large group of tongues. In surveying Pound's early career one hardly knows whether to be more astonished at the inaccuracy of his knowledge or the wideness of its range. His first book of verse *A Lume Spento* contains some startling illiteracies. The student of Romance languages had not even a schoolboy's competence in Latin. Yet in a few years he was to write a book called *The Spirit of Romance,* which is a series of glimpses of Romance literature from the *Pervigilium Veneris,* through medieval Latin, Provençal, early Italian and Spanish to old French. It has not any particular scholarly value and does not pretend to it, but it is even now an extremely attractive, lively, first-hand account of the divers works that it describes.

Pound is after all very clear about what he wants. He cares for poetry, and he wants only such knowledge as a practising poet can directly use. His attitude is one of glad discipleship to a variety of foreign literatures. He is followed in this by Eliot, much more discreetly. The rather self-consciously cosmopolitan air that we find in Mr. Eliot's early poems and in *The Waste Land* is to be found too in *Harmonium,* the first volume of Wallace Stevens. It is noticeable that the distinguished critic of this generation, Mr. Edmund Wilson, regards this internationalism as the character of the literary scene even today. In a recent interview published in the London *Sunday Times* he remarked, "The whole world is getting to be more alike in certain ways. We're all having to deal with more or less the same kind of society, so that national literatures and all that are becoming less important."[7] It is in some such faith that the polyglot mosaic of the later *Cantos,* and possibly *Finnegans Wake,* appear to have been composed.

Our literary revolution, then, is a cosmopolitan affair. Biographically speaking it is a revolution of expatriates and exiles; and this is so before and quite apart from the enforced exile brought about by revolution and war. It is an age of arbitrary migrations and displacements. Henry James, in this as in other ways, is the father of much in modern Anglo-American letters. Eliot follows him in turning his back on the American scene and ultimately adopting English nationality. Pound's active years were spent in London, Paris and Rapallo, and he was never again in his own country until he re-entered it in tragic and problematical circumstances after the last war. Joyce deliberately elects a career of "silence, exile and cunning," has no other theme but Dublin, yet writes of it in memory from Trieste, Zurich and Paris. Lawrence after writing one great novel straight out of his native experience spends the rest of his life in restless wandering over the world in search of somewhere to settle. And in a younger generation Auden reverses the usual course of literary migration and leaves England to settle in America. Yeats is almost alone among the great writers of the early part of this century in writing out of the heart of his own country.

This cosmopolitanism may be simply accepted and embraced as an essential part of the contemporary scene. Edmund Wilson seems to take it in this way, and there are many who have been willing to extend and generalise the idea. Geographical eclecticism has gone hand in hand with historical eclecticism, and both have been extended to other arts than literature. André Malraux founds his art-criticism on the idea of the "imaginary museum." The modern painter, thanks to the technical advance that has made improved methods of reproduction possible, and thanks too to history and anthropology, has at his disposal the whole body of painting of all times and all countries, so that his relation to the past is radically different from that of any of his predecessors. There has been no comparable technical revolution affecting literature, and the great un-international fact of language forbids it; but the enormous diffusion of historical and anthropological knowledge has had something of the same effect—as the Great Books courses bear witness. And Mr. Donald

Davie, with some qualifications, has suggested that
the modern poet too lives in an imaginary museum,
and that his writing is inevitably affected by it.[8] He
must proceed by pastiche and allusion, and must
acknowledge by nods and becks and lifted eyebrows
his awareness "that there are modes of experience or
ways of saying things which the poet is aware of
though his poem on its own account is not." Mr.
Davie makes this a recommendation; it seems to me
a concise recipe for some of the most meretricious
effects in modern poetry; but his way of thinking is
obviously relevant to the poetry of the last fifty years.

We can consider this denationalisation of the literary scene in another way. We can consider the audience. The audience for literature in English has no
longer any homogeneity, except that provided by
its tendency to read literature written in English.
Its members may live in Edinburgh or Hampstead
or Brooklyn or Seattle or Sydney, or quite possibly
Jamaica or Bombay. No community of experience can
possibly be assumed between them. We can see this
most clearly by thinking of the destiny of the novel,
since the direct mimesis of experience is more in the
foreground there than in any other form. The typical
situation through the eighteenth and nineteenth centuries was the assumption of a shared experience
between writer and reader. The reader of Fielding
or Dickens was assumed and on the whole rightly

assumed to be as much in possession of the social data and the literary conventions on which the novel was founded as the writer himself. The English reader of Faulkner is commonly quite uninformed about the world Faulkner portrays, or rather about what sort of relation the novels have to historical reality. He reads him as he reads Dostoievski. He presumes that behind Faulkner's imaginative vision lies a world and a society, but it is one that is wholly mysterious to him, apart from the novels themselves. I persuade myself that I see a similar situation in Lionel Trilling's study of Forster; Professor Trilling sees his subject as a moralist in a dateless, unlocalised sense, or relates him to broad general currents of ideas; while an English reader must I think always start his appreciation of Mr. Forster (it will not conclude there) with a vivid sense of his contact with a particular social life, and his provenance from a specialised cultural milieu. It is no use approving or deploring this state of things; it is simply there. For writers like Faulkner and Forster, each of whom has been able to write out of a specific culture, it will merely mean a diversity of readings. For the writer who is aware of his large denationalised potential audience, the situation is different. It offers temptations—the temptation to exploit by snob-appeal a false assumption of common experience; or to exploit by a kind of bullying exoticism the absence of community. It can happen with Hemingway. We are asked to agree that we are all friendly with head-waiters and very good at bullfighting. Yes, we reply, with a false complicity, we are like that too: or alternatively, in abject submission, No, we are not like that at all; we lead very quiet lives; do tell us Mr. Hemingway, you are so clever and so brave. There is a kind of impurity here, both in the reaction of the audience and in the fact that it has been played for; an impurity not caused but probably much encouraged by the huge international swamp of readers to which such a writer appeals.

So that I cannot regard the detribalisation of literature with much complacency. I doubt whether the Anglo-American literary community is a real community, or that any particular effort should be kept up to make it so. I believe that a writer today should be suspicious of any attempt to appeal to the vast faceless international audience. It may be that he has no community left. It is a melancholy thing that one of the most moving of all sonnets, "Heureux qui comme Ulysse," can so often now be no more than the motive to a historical regret. There is no *pays* to return to. But I think we should try to make one, and that the writer should, so far as it is in his power, write from and for those whom he knows, whose habits and experiences he shares. It will be the best chance he has of bringing something living to those whose experiences he does not share.

The Nature of a Revolution

And this brings me back to the poetic revolution of the childhood of the century, to its singularly rootless character. Many of the great works of modern literature seem to exist in a vacuum, to spring from no particular society and to address no particular audience. *The Waste Land* is founded on a vegetation myth that is universal rather than particular. It draws its religious symbolism from Buddhism and the Upanishads as well as from Christianity. Since this poem aims at a kind of comprehensiveness and universality the feeling of non-attachment to any particular cultural context is wholly appropriate. *Finnegans Wake,* in spite of its obsessive attachment to Howth Castle and environs, aims to represent nothing less than the total dream of man, so it too must be based on a universal resurrection myth, and deserting any one language descend into the mind's workshop where language itself is formed. These are highly idiosyncratic encyclopedic successes; as the *Cantos* is an idiosyncratic encyclopedic failure. In any case their being depends on their encyclopedic quality. The smaller forms need a more precise focus. Eliot's early quasi-satirical poems and the satirical pieces in Pound's *Ripostes* and *Lustra* both suffer from the lack of it. Burbank with his Baedeker, Bleistein with his cigar, Mr. Hecatomb Styrax and the Milwins hardly seem more aimless, clueless and unattached than the lyric speakers who reflect on their condition. Satire needs a firm social base. The violently energetic, cruelly trenchant pamphleteering of Wyndham Lewis, locally so powerful that one begins to think of a comparison with Swift, never makes its full effect as a whole because it has no consistent standpoint, no basis in society or intellectual tradition. There is a similar spirit in criticism. Its main symptoms are a continual talk about the European tradition, and a continual unwillingness to accept the canon of European letters as it is. There was an itch to be continually tinkering with reputations, usually in a destructive fashion—to hound out Virgil or Petrarch, to dislodge Milton, to make it impossible for any right-thinking person to read Shelley, or whatever it might be. All such attempts to erase sanctified names from the public monuments are symptoms of insecurity. I try to say this neutrally. Probably things could not have been other than they were; I am only concerned to remark on what they were.

The general cultural cosmopolitanism that I have been trying to observe, strongly reinforced in our case by the presence of two powerful American writers who felt themselves to be intellectual citizens of the world, can be seen—indeed I cannot help seeing it—as in some sense opposed to the English literary tradition. It is hard to find the right shade of definition in talking of this. Of course the English poetic tradition has been from the start a matter of continual influence from Latin culture—mostly from France but nearly as much from Italy. Often a native growth has been opposed by a highly authoritative influence from abroad, and the two have had to be reconciled in a new synthesis. One thinks of the problem Dryden and the neo-classic critics had in reconciling the presence of Shakespeare with the formal ideals of drama derived from France. But then Shakespeare himself would be unthinkable without the great body of Romance literature from which he drew much of his material. And so it has always gone on. This continual and extremely civilised dialogue has been the very substance of the English literary tradition. Of all men Pound appeared to be the most vociferously aware of it. ("All English poetry is a history of successful steals from the French," he said.) Yet he is curiously unaware of its real nature. In his early days Pound was an indefatigable propagandist for Provençal poetry and its value as a technical example to the English verse of his time. But he hardly seems to recognise that English poetry had begun to absorb the Provençal lessons in the thirteenth century, that whatever was relevant in them had long since passed into English poetics. That is perhaps why his own verse on Provençal themes has so much the air of Rossetti and the nineties; he is not really learning anything that he did not learn from existing English lyric verse. What comes out is the style of his own day, or the day before; though of course he is writing it with his own immense personal distinction. The programme for the aspirant English poet or student of poetry outlined in *How to Read*[9] neglects all the process of gradual growth and assimilation that has made up poetry in English, neglects all the slow, thorough absorption that is necessary for a real education, and would substitute a huge barbaric indigestible meal of gobbets. Pound's energy and enthusiasm, his impatient fury to extend the range of twentieth-century poetic vision, are extremely sympathetic qualities:

> English and American culture of the generation preceding mine, and the completely contemptible and damnable activity of the literary bureaucracy in power . . . has been occupied chiefly with the inane assertion of the non-existence of the giraffe, and *magari* not of the giraffe alone, but of whole tribes of animals, the puma, the panther, the well-known Indian buffalo.[10]

Yes, indeed; but the implied analogy of a poetic tradition with a menagerie is not a happy one. It is surely a good thing to know something of the variety of the animal creation; but if you live in Norfolk there is not much sense in breeding pumas and panthers; except as isolated curiosities it is necessary to stick to what suits your soil and climate. The lunatic jumble of asyntactical English, tags of Latin, Greek, Italian, German and French, interspersed with Chinese ideograms which have neither auditory nor conceptual significance for the Western reader—this kind of thing in the later cantos is an extreme projection of the eclecticism Pound exhibits at the start. And if one is for better or worse a writer in the English language a continual crotchety hostility to the English poetic tradition is a poor ground for experiment. I trust it is not an offended provincialism that speaks. I have never been in a position to hold the whole of European literature from Homer in the mind; but I have cared for the Latin and Italian poetry that I know as much as any, and I have been as devoted to French poetry as to English: it is for this very reason that the barbarous tasteless hewing up of gobbets, the gross jumbling of incompatible fragments seems so offensive. It is surely astonishing that Pound and Eliot, the two poets of our day who have shown themselves most sensitive to rhythm, and have done the most to quicken a sense of linguistic decorum, should have practised so much insertion of unacclimatised and undigested fragments into their work. It is a curious experience to hear Mr. Eliot's own reading of *The Waste Land,* and, every time we arrive at one of the quotations in a foreign language—*Frisch weht der Wind/ Der Heimat zu,* or *Et O ces voix d'enfants, chantant dans la coupole!* —even though the concession is made of pronouncing them all pretty uniformly after the school of Stratford-atte-Bowe, to note the hideously awkward gear-change, the intrusion of an alien rhythm and an alien vowel-system, into verse otherwise distinguished by the fineness of its auditory imagination. It is a curious thing that Joyce, perhaps the most technically accomplished master of every variety of English prose that we have ever seen, should conclude his career with the polyglot jargon of *Finnegans Wake*. It is almost heartbreaking when the gibberish is compared with the breath-taking beauty and power of some of the intervening passages that are still written in an accessible language.

This is meant as criticism of the past, not as present polemic, for this phase of experiment has gone by. But it is perhaps a symptom of some more general condition in the revolutionary literature of this century. Every great spiritual change demands in the end a change of idiom, rhythm and poetic method to compare with it. But the technical developments can occur without being the response to any deep movement of the spirit. The changes begun by Wordsworth and Coleridge were the technical counterparts to a great revolution in philosophy and general outlook—the change from a philosophy of mechanism to one of organism. That is why the Romantic movement is such a massive and inescapable fact, even to those who dislike its ideas and some of their literary manifestations. I do not believe that the poetic revolution of the twentieth century is a fact of the same order. It was not a spiritual revolution. The Romantic movement left a legacy of feelings and ideas to the whole nineteenth century. I can see no sign that such an inheritance has come down from the great literary figures of the twenties. They had nothing to leave. Their revolution was one of technique and sensibility, not a movement of the spirit in any profound sense. Coleridge talks of Wordsworth's union of deep feeling with profound thought. Mr. Eliot's characteristic doctrine is that the poet does not think, and need not personally feel—though happily his own thoughtful and deeply felt poetry belies his principles. Joyce seems to have had no development, no attachment, no beliefs outside his art; all is contained within an intricate technical code. Pound's early poetry suffers from the lack of an adequate subject-matter; it too often seems to be technical experiment in a void: there are a few climactic moments when matter and accomplishment come together; then all is dissipated in a waste of sterile eccentricity. It is notable that the two great writers of this period who are least interested in novelty of technique, Yeats and Lawrence, are the two whose work reveals a continual spiritual quest.

To return for a moment to Mr. Eliot's notion that the poet does not think. "It is the general notion of 'thinking' that I would challenge. . . . Did Shakespeare think at all? He was occupied in turning human actions into poetry."[11] The whole passage deserves careful consideration. One must take it to mean that it is not the business of the poet as such to be a "thinker." He may take over his "thought" bodily from his age, or from other writers; and in any case his poetic quality will be independent of the philosophical value of his thinking. This is the kind of argument that is formally hard to refute, yet seems to be leading in the wrong direction. It marks a tendency in modern discussion of poetry—the tendency to underplay the role of poetic thought. What gives Romantic poetry as a whole its strong, deep and steady movement is not only that it was part of a more inclusive movement in thought, politics and society; it is also that the most living questions of the age were actually worked out in poetry. Poetry was the medium in which the poets did their thinking. This is strikingly true of Wordsworth, Keats and Shelley, less true of Coleridge, but true again of Byron so far as he thought at all. In reading *The Prelude,* Keats's *Odes* and the two *Hyperions,* or *Prometheus Unbound,* one is conscious of thought that profoundly affects the poet and his fellows, actually being worked out in the process of writing the poetry. One who has read these works, even if he had read nothing else, has felt much of the force and pressure of the age. A reader of the characteristic modern works — shall we say *The Waste Land, Hugh Selwyn Mauberley* and *Ulysses?* — will have experienced something far more peripheral, something that cannot take him, as the works of the Romantic poets can, close to the very centre of the time. It will be said of Mr. Eliot that his poetry, especially after *The Waste Land,* is the record of a developing spiritual experience, and that its thought is both central and deeply felt. And this is true. But it is true in a very special sense. Faithful to his own critical insight, Mr. Eliot does not "think" in this poetry. He is following a traditional and well-tried road, not exploring a new region. The poetic ordonnance is his own, handled with a beautiful sensitiveness and invention; but the underlying structure of the thought is something discovered not devised; and it has been discovered and expounded many times before. The numerous quotations from the liturgy and the spiritual classics bear witness to this. There is thought and there is poetry; but they are not part of the same process. The poetry is not in the thought and the thought in the poetry in the *Four Quartets* as it is in the *Odes* of Keats.

It is the absence of any deep current of thought, any massive and widely shared direction of the spirit that throws so much of the emphasis of modern literary activity on technique and formal experiment. Pound's idea of the study of literature as the study of technical invention is the most extraordinary case in point. The shrewdness and wit of the technical comment in his pamphlet *How to Read,* the tinny assertiveness of everything else, shows up the paradox in its sharpest form. But in many other places a rift can be observed between means employed and total end proposed— technical experiment pursued for its own sake and no longer controlled by any central purpose. The best illustration is *Ulysses,* manifestly a work of genius but almost unique among works of comparable scale in ice-bound self-containedness, the absence of any view of life, of any ethic or metaphysic, asserted or implied. What is there instead? An immense system of correspondences, elaborate literary and symbolic parallels. This is the system that is exposed in Stuart Gilbert's study (we can take it as authoritative since it is derived from Joyce himself), where each of the eighteen episodes of *Ulysses* is paralleled to an episode of the *Odyssey,* and has besides its particular hour, organ of the body, art, colour, symbol and technique. It can safely be said that no one would have been aware of these correspondences as elements in the pattern, except in the vaguest and most fragmentary way, unless he had been informed of them from the outside. Yet this sterile elaboration is a real part of the structure. Or we can take the Oxen of the Sun episode—that is the scene in the lying-in hospital—where the process of embryonic development is paralleled in a series of pastiches of every notable prose style in English from the Anglo-Saxon chronicle to Walter Pater. Brilliant writing, one can imagine no one else who could have done it—but in the end a device, an ingenious piece of machinery and nothing more. And of course I am selecting only obvious examples; the student of Joyce could illustrate the use of wanton intricate ingenuities *ad infinitum.*

The Nature of a Revolution

After the Romantic movement had done its work, the relation of man to nature, the relation of man to man, were all changed, all different from what they had been before. The change was brought about by forces that to a large degree worked through literature, and in any case were expressed in it. The great forces at work in the early twentieth century do not realise themselves in literature to anything like the same extent. If the young man of 1840 was different from the young man of 1800 the main reasons were Wordsworth and Byron. If the young man of 1940 was different from the young man of 1900 the main reasons were Marx and Freud. We noticed earlier that Romantic modes of feeling and expression were a model for three succeeding generations; and that our twentieth-century revolution already seems to have exhausted a large part of its influence. There are technical reasons for this that we have tried to suggest; some of the typical experiments of the twenties are specialised, inimitable, perhaps in the end self-annihilating. But we can now discern a much larger and more general reason for the restricted influence of the new poetry. It was not the vehicle of a great spiritual force; it did not have behind it the flow and impetus of a great movement of society and ideas. It may be that literature will never have this power again; it is perhaps through the sciences, or the pseudo-sciences of psychology and sociology that these forces will express themselves; and that literature will be the vehicle not of ideas or the great streams of feeling, but merely of the sensibilities. We have so little notion of what our society is going to look like in fifty years' time that it is useless to speculate.

To take a shorter view, we might ask ourselves what developments have outlived the revolutionary decade, and what changes in the poetic landscape have been effected. There are a number of signs in England of an attempt to return to some pre-lapsarian innocence. In poetry and in talk about poetry, in the novel and in talk about the novel, a half-defiant parochialism is set up against the cosmopolitanism of the preceding age; and in this I may be thought to share, though it is not my intention. Two influential novelists of the present generation who are not at all parochial but very much men of the world, Mr. Angus Wilson and Sir Charles Snow, have expressed or implied or suggested a large lack of interest in the experimental fiction of the twenties and thirties; their suasions are towards the large-scale socially-oriented novel, the presentation of the world as it actually works, without any fiddle-faddle about form and verbal nicety. This too may begin to sound like some of the things I have been saying; but it is only a parody of them, and I wish to detach myself from it as delicately as I can. Personally I find the ethics and social attitude of Henry James anti-pathetic; the achievements of Joyce are probably quite unrepeatable; the sensibility of Virginia Woolf seems dangerously specialised and limited. Yet I believe that the novel will only continue as a serious form of art by learning whatever it can from these writers, and applying it, inevitably, to different social and human material. The social-descriptive tradition of the novel, the emphasis on mimesis rather than on the creation of something that is satisfying in itself by its form and texture, has had a long and honourable run in English. The novel has often got on pretty comfortably without much self-consciousness in formal matters; but I doubt if it can do so again. It may be in just this field that the new pseudo-sciences begin to encroach on literary preserves. The striking success of such books as *The Lonely Crowd* and *The Organization Man,* abominably written as they mostly are, and lacking any conceivable appeal to the emotions and the sensibilities, seems to suggest that the appetite for this kind of examination of society may be satisfied outside the field of art altogether. If we are to have great slabs of social realism they may as well be simply real. For over sixty years (much longer if we think of France) there has been a growing sense of prose fiction as something that must combine adequacy to experience with its own kind of formal perfection; something that can be still prose but can work with some of the subtlety and directness of poetry. The rise of this sense coincides with the decline of the long poem. No one writes epics now, and if they did no one would read them. The novel has taken their place. And it feels the need of the refinement of structure and texture that poetry has acquired in its longer and more arduous career. If the novel were to continue on the lines of *Finnegans Wake* and *The Waves* it would soon cease to exist: if it were to refuse to learn what can be learnt from them it might as well cease.

The remark about the novel and the long poem brings me to a larger but related matter. The boundaries between prose and verse are no longer so clear as they were. The important division seems to come in another place. This is partly a technical affair. The practice of free verse, which is in essence an attempt to isolate a personal organic, meditative rhythm, without reference to any of the accepted metrical patterns, comes to coincide with the careful and self-conscious organisation of prose. They have worked together to make the distinction often merely typographical. Apart from their appearance on the page parts of *Finnegans Wake* are much like what we used to call verse, parts of the *Four Quartets* much like what we used to call prose. But there is a more than technical reason. The immense expansion and prestige of the natural sciences, the extension of scientific method to more or less humane studies, has meant that the real dividing line in our discourse comes now not between prose and verse, but between any writing organised for an aes-

thetic purpose and all other kinds of writing whatso-
ever. This fact has been widely recognised in the criticism of the last forty years, and the dichotomy between
"scientific" and "emotive" writing, with a variety of
terminology, has been widely employed. It was recognised already by Mallarmé in 1895 when he wrote that
the form called verse is simply literature itself; it begins
as soon as there is any conscious attempt at style. This
remains true although *vers libre* is little practised in
English today. In what is called formal verse at the
moment there is in fact a considerable approximation
to the rhythms of prose; and prose of any but the
humblest pretensions will not easily forget, or be for-
given if it does, the refined orchestration of the great
formalists.

I have left to the last the most considerable and certain of the legacies of the earlier modern poetry—the
establishment of a modern poetic diction. It is largely
the work of Mr. Eliot, whose constant concern it has
been. He has adapted the oft-quoted phrase of Mallarmé, and said of himself and his friends that it was
their concern "to purify the language of the tribe." In
another place he has said that the creation of a proper
modern poetic idiom was the task of poetry in the early
part of the century; and the passages on language in
the *Four Quartets* show how enduringly he has been
engaged with this matter. This is the greatest exception to what has been said up to now about the

intractability of imagist poetry as a model. Here Eliot's writing, both in practice and in theory, has been a decisive influence—not by generating direct imitation, but by the much better way of guiding and informing taste and providing some impeccable but not easily imitable examples. And the lesson has been learnt; the new sense of decorum about poetic language that it has inculcated has become almost too acute. It makes difficulties with an obviously great poet like Hardy whose control of diction is obviously uncertain. Perhaps we are becoming too squeamish; but if so it is an evidence of how far the chastening of our poetic idiom has gone. Recent writing tends to speak as though this had always been a conscious preoccupation of poets, but it is hardly so. The Elizabethans seem to have been only intermittently conscious of the question of poetic diction, and the Romantics after Wordsworth hardly conscious of it at all. Nineteenth-century poetic idiom seems to have grown up almost without conscious criticism; and the praetorian cohorts of Romantic verse were a fairly disorderly band by the time they came to be demobilised in the earlier part of this century. It was at that time that the idea of a poetic language based on living speech was revived. Ford Madox Ford was a great propagandist for it, and Pound, whose diction up to the time he met Ford was of the purest Wardour-Street school, seems to have taken up the doctrine from him; and it became of course a part of Imagist doctrine. But to talk of a poetic language based on living speech is in itself little more than a pious aspiration. Actually to create such a language, and to make it not only contemporary and alive, but also rich and flexible enough for all the purposes that poetry requires—that is a very different matter. Mr. Eliot achieved it at a very early stage in his career. Some of the irony of *Prufrock* has faded, and the stanza poems of 1920 seem by now rather insecure; yet in all of them the precision of the language in general, the judiciously evocative phrases, never allowed to get out of hand, the sparing and controlled richness, are all as valid examples still as at the time of their first appearance. But he has described these ideals of language himself:

> The common word exact without vulgarity,
> The formal word precise but not pedantic,
> The whole consort dancing together.

And this, or something like it on a lower level of accomplishment, is a piece of craftsmanship that younger poets have been able to learn. There is neither a metric, nor a rhetoric, nor a subject-matter today that has become traditional and generally available, but there is a diction.

So the poetry of the present and the immediate future has not been too richly endowed by its predecessors, but neither has it been left destitute. There are no indubitable prophets among its fathers, so it has inherited no body of extra-literary doctrine; and this is perhaps not a misfortune; the too-easy availability of Wordsworthian natural religion was not a certain blessing to the nineteenth century. As I have tried to show, poetry has been left a good deal of machinery that it cannot use; but it has also been left a set of admirable tools, still sharp, still usable, still unimpaired by having been turned to meaner purposes.

At this point I should like to call up the shade of Hardy, the last great writer both in prose and verse to stand wholly outside the modern movement. His life just overlaps the early years of modern literature with which we have been concerned, but of course his formation belongs entirely to an earlier age. By looking at his work we can get some idea of what English writing has gained and what it has lost in our century. It is hard to imagine a novelist of his stature today who would not be free of his more obvious defects. Bad writing we have always with us, but the peculiar kind of bad writing that is often found in Hardy—the stiffness, the polysyllabic humour, the pseudo-scientific jargon, the dialogue that is neither natural nor stylised, but merely artificial—these would hardly be tolerated in the present age. Nor would the abuse of coincidence, the feeling that the novel had been written to a thesis instead of according to its own internal development. Since Hardy's time we have come to demand that language should be a more responsive instrument, and that fiction should work through it, not merely employ it as a necessary but unconsidered means. And yet in the end none of this seems to matter very much; no one feels that Hardy's stature is ultimately affected by what we can only label his deficiencies. The images of acting, feeling and suffering human beings are too deeply felt and too powerfully communicated for our consciousness of a clumsy method to be more than a critical afterthought. His knowledge of his own world is both intimate and profound. It is a local rustic world, but by knowing and feeling it to the core Hardy has made it also into the image of the great world. Without the aid of fertility rituals or the collective unconscious he has shown how the provincial can become the universal.

His poetry triumphs over obstacles in the same way. Here the obstacles are even more marked. By the current criterion of a chastened and accomplished diction many of them are put out of court at once. The reader is tripped up on ponderous pieces of scientific vocabulary; archaisms abound, not used purposively, but simply as convenient chunks of ready-made poetics; syntax is distorted to fit a metre and words are dragged in to make a rhyme. None of the accomplished younger poets of the mid-century, disciplined and made conscious of their craft by the Imagist regimen, would be guilty of such gaucheries. Yet again the triumph occurs—partly for the same reasons as in the novels, reasons that have more to do with humanity and vision than technique. But there is another reason too, the ever present lyricism, a very varied, meditative yet musical rhythm, something extremely personal, apparently unstudied; through which we nevertheless hear the centuries-old voice of English Lyric poetry. It is notable and touching to see Pound paying his tribute to one whose attitude to poetry was at the opposite pole to his own. Pound wrote of Hardy in a letter of 1922: "He woke one to the extent of his own absorption in *subject* as contrasted with aesthetes' preoccupation with 'treatment.' "[12] And again in 1933: "The old man's road (*vide* Tom. Hardy) CONTENT, the INSIDES, the subject matter."[13]

This points us in another direction from formal refinement and purifying the language of the tribe. Yet there seems no reason why the two directions should be permanently opposed. The early poetic exercises of the modern movement were a discipline, an askesis, conducted almost without regard to the purpose for which the training was undertaken. But weight-reducing and body-building are tedious performances unless the stripped and strengthened body is going to be used for something. And of course it has been; but no thanks to the prevalent poetic theory. Doctrines that would make meaning merely a sop to the intellect, distil poetry to a pure invisible essence, purge it of the taint of personality, all have their value, but in the end become confining and sterilising. In the famous essay in which the impersonal theory of poetry is announced Mr. Eliot wrote, speaking of the relation of the poet to his work:

> I shall, therefore, invite you to consider, as a suggestive analogy, the action that takes place when a bit of finely filiated platinum is introduced into a chamber containing oxygen and sulphur dioxide.[14]

We are puzzled by this; but before the suspense becomes intolerable we are given the answer: sulphurous acid is produced, and the platinum remains unchanged. The analogy we are invited to consider is that of the catalyst—a substance in whose presence alone a chemical reaction takes place, but which itself does not participate in the reaction and remains unaffected by it. So should the poet behave; the argument concludes, "The mind of the poet is the shred of platinum."

The language of criticism is frequently metaphorical. We need not deplore this, and we can learn much from attending to the metaphors. For certain purposes and at a certain historical point it was doubtless very apt and very salutary to liken the poet to a finely filiated bit of platinum. At the present conjunction of the stars it might also be well to remember the quite unmetaphorical saying of an earlier writer—that the poet is a man speaking to men.

NOTES

I. Imagism and Its Consequences

1 *Literary Essays of Ezra Pound* (London, 1954), pp. 6, 11.

2 *Ibid.,* p. xi.

3 R. P. Blackmur, *Anni Mirabiles 1921-25* (Washington, 1956), p. 41.

4 *Literary Essays of Ezra Pound,* pp. 5, 9.

5 W. B. Yeats, *Essays* (London, 1924), p. 142.

6 Stéphane Mallarmé, *Œuvres Complètes* (Pleiade, Paris, 1945), p. 368.

7 Copyright 1926 by Ezra Pound. Reprinted by permission of *New Directions.*

8 "The Approach to Paris," *The New Age,* Oct. 2, 1913.

9 Copyright 1926 by Ezra Pound. Reprinted by permission of *New Directions.*

10 *Literary Essays of Ezra Pound,* pp. 5, 6, 17.

11 James Joyce, *Stephen Hero* (New York, 1955), p. 210.

12 "Hamlet and His Problems," *The Sacred Wood* (London, 1920), p. 100.

13 T. S. Eliot, *The Use of Poetry and the Use of Criticism* (London, 1933), p. 151.

14 From *Anabase* by St.-John Perse, translated by T. S. Eliot, copyright 1938, 1949, by Harcourt, Brace and Company, Inc., and reprinted with their permission. Throughout, the quotations from T. S. Eliot's *Collected Poems* (copyright 1936, by Harcourt, Brace and Company, Inc.) are used by permission of the publishers.

15 See *Letters of Ezra Pound* (New York, 1950), pp. 169-172. It is also noteworthy that in John Rodker's circular for Bel Esprit, a proposed literary fund, *The Waste Land* is referred to as "a series of poems." (*Letters of Ezra Pound,* p. 175).

16 Grover Smith, *T. S. Eliot's Poetry and Plays* (Chicago, 1956), p. 58.

17 *Ibid.,* p. 58. See also George Williamson, *A Reader's Guide to T. S. Eliot* (New York, 1957), p. 123.

II. Imagist Poetry and the Tradition

1 *Essays in Criticism,* III, Jan. 1953, p. 2.

2 Note contributed by Pound to *The Townsman,* Jan. 1938. Quoted in Hugh Kenner, *The Poetry of Ezra Pound* (London, 1951), p. 309.

3 T. E. Hulme, *Speculations* (London, 1936), pp. 111-141. The references following are all to this essay.

Notes

4 T. S. Eliot, *After Strange Gods* (London, 1934), p. 3.

5 T. S. Eliot, *The Idea of a Christian Society* (London, 1940), p. 27.

6 Robert Frost, *Complete Poems* (New York, 1949), p. 279.

7 C. S. Lewis, *De Descriptione Temporum* (Cambridge, 1955), p. 14.

8 *Essays in Criticism, op. cit.*, pp. 345-357.

9 J. Campbell and H. M. Robinson, *A Skeleton Key to Finnegans Wake* (London, 1947), p. 295.

10 Kenner, *op. cit.*, p. 91.

11 R. P. Blackmur, *Language as Gesture* (New York, 1935), p. 54.

12 Kenner, *op. cit.*, p. 194.

13 René Taupin, *L'Influence du Symbolisme Français sur la Poésie Americaine, 1910-1920* (Paris, 1929).

14 Elizabeth Sewell, *The Structure of Poetry* (London, 1951), p. 144.

15 M. H. Abrams, review of Frank Kermode's *Romantic Image* in *Victorian Studies*, Sept. 1958, p. 77.

III. The Nature of a Revolution

1 Quoted in M. Cunliffe, *The Literature of the United States* (London, 1954), p. 9.

2 Ralph Waldo Emerson, "The Poet," 1844.

3 Walt Whitman, Preface to *Leaves of Grass*, 1855.

4 Walt Whitman, *Democratic Vistas*, 1871.

5 Ralph Waldo Emerson, "The Poet."

6 Richard Chase, *The American Novel and its Tradition* (New York, 1957), p. ix.

7 *The Sunday Times*, Feb. 1, 1959.

8 *The Listener*, July 12, 1957.

9 *Literary Essays of Ezra Pound*, pp. 15-41.

10 *Ibid.*, p. 78.

11 T. S. Eliot, *Selected Essays* (London, 1932), p. 115.

12 *Letters of Ezra Pound*, p. 178.

13 *Ibid.*, p. 248.

14 T. S. Eliot, *The Sacred Wood* (London, 1920), p. 53.